FUNKNOLOGY

FUNKNOLOGY

A Synthesis of Art, Science, and Being

Jimi Calhoun

CASCADE *Books* · Eugene, Oregon

FUNKNOLOGY
A Synthesis of Art, Science, and Being

Cascade Books
An Imprint of Wipf and Stock Publishers
199 W. 8th Ave., Suite 3
Eugene, OR 97401

www.wipfandstock.com

PAPERBACK ISBN: 978-1-7252-8723-5
HARDCOVER ISBN: 978-1-7252-8724-2
EBOOK ISBN: 978-1-7252-8725-9

Cataloguing-in-Publication data:

Names: Calhoun, Jimi, author.

Title: Funknology : a synthesis of art, science, and being / Jimi Calhoun.

Description: Eugene, OR: Cascade Books, 2021 | Includes bibliographical references.

Identifiers: ISBN 978-1-7252-8723-5 (paperback) | ISBN 978-1-7252-8724-2 (hardcover) | ISBN 978-1-7252-8725-9 (ebook)

Subjects: LCSH: Race relations—Religious aspects—Christianity. | Funk (Music). | African Americans—Music—History and criticism.

Classification: E185.615 .C26.5 2021 (paperback) | E185.615 (ebook)

11/05/21

Dedicated to
Cheryl Nancy Faye, Mike Goodman, and Sidney George, Jr.

In loving memory of
William and Xanthyne Calhoun and Jules and Lorraine Brown

CONTENTS

ACKNOWLEDGMENTS

To my rock, Julaine, who contributes so much to everything I do. You have rolled with every twist and turn life has thrown our way; you are amazing. To my extended family and friends: thank you.

I am grateful for the funk musicians I have been fortunate enough to have been involved with in one setting or another. You have contributed much to this funknology: Clifford Coulter, John Turk, Billy Ingram, Arthur Chavez, Jr., Reynaldo Guzman, Douglas Ingram, Napoleon Murphy Brock, Jerry Perez, Clark Baldwin, Louis Oros, Wayne Bartlett, Leon Patillo, Neil Stallings, Carol Stallings, Dennis Marcellino, Joe Provost, Lenny Lee Goldsmith, Barry "Frosty" Smith, Cornelius Bumpus, Jr., Snooky Flowers, Bobby Freeman, Sly Stone, Jerry Martini, Greg Errico, Cynthia Robinson, Ron E. Beck, Mel Brown, Dr. John, John Boudreaux, Freddie Staehle, David Sanborn, Buzzy Feiten, Sterling Spell, Alvin Robinson, Jessie Smith, Robbie Montgomery, Jerry Jumonville, Darryl Leonard, James Booker, Gene Redding, Jimmy McGhee, Eddie Tuduri, Joanne Vent, Etta James, Lou Rawls, George Clinton, Eddie Hazel, Buddy Miles, Jimi Hendrix, Martha Reeves, Levi Stubbs, Abdul "Duke" Fakir, Renaldo "Obie" Benson and Lawrence Payton, Ray Monette, Chet McCracken, Jerry La Croix, Eddie Guzman, Frank Westbrook, Gil Bridges, Sidney George, Travis Fullerton, and Dennis Kenmore. Thank you.

I am indebted to the churches and faith communities that have helped shape my thinking along the journey: Hope Chapel, Bridging Austin, The Iona Community, the Foursquare Church, the Presbyterian Church, the Anglican Communion, North American and American Baptist churches, the Roman Catholic Church, Gateway, and the W-H Gordon Life Group. I would not be the minister I am without you.

INTRODUCTION

This is a book about Funk from a musician's perspective, and Funk with a sociological and theological application. Taken together they become a medium for reconciliation that *The Oxford Dictionary* defines as "the action of making one view or belief compatible with another."[1] What is written on the pages that follow is the result of many years of studying theology as a minister, in combination with years of playing bass professionally in Funk bands, hence the title *Funknology*. Funknology was born out of the living conditions that people of African descent have experienced as a diasporic community, as seen through the eyes of a musical artist and a pastor. Funknology asserts the positives situated in Black culture in rebuttal to the negative stereotypes placed upon us due to our outsider status. When writing about how African American Jews face discrimination in white Jewish spaces, Nylah Burton said, "People cannot thrive in communities that intrinsically sees them as outsiders."[2] That describes the lives that the vast majority of Black people in America have lived since they arrived on these shores.

One of my aims for this book is to confront the complexities of race relations and then take on one of the most urgent questions of our time, "How should we live together?" American history is one of racial separation and it is not that different today. The great New Orleans musician Dr. John once quipped, "What is, is connected to what was." Author Graeme Nicholson noted, "A people that lives in history, moves in it."[3] And African theologian Peter J. Paris wrote, "Historical experience shapes the nature

---

1. Lexico.com, "Reconciliation," line 2.
2. Burton, "Black Jews," para. 5.
3. Nicholson, *Justifying*, 132.

of theology and ethics."[4] Funknology is an extension of Black historical experience. I will be pulling insights from history throughout these pages because the truth about the character and morality of a country, and its people, must include *all* of their stories. It is important to remember that history can be more than meets the proverbial eye. It was an interpretation of events when it was written—and it is interpreted in certain ways when it is being read. Through the synthesizing of art, science, and religion, Funknology will help you better understand Black history in the context of the Black lived experience.

There are many who are comfortable living with a misconception that religion cannot provide satisfying answers to the question about how we can live together in peace. They are of the opinion that politics, education, economics, or science can provide answers, but not religion. I am arguing that it is time to reclaim the word *religion* from the metaphorical trash bin of pejorative characterizations, and restore it to its rightful place among other positive influences on culture. The third section of this book is written with the belief that religion—rather than simply being a divisive force as some have argued—is by definition conciliatory in nature because the root word of religion means to "bind . . . unite."[5] And the ultimate goal of this book is to unite Blacks, whites, and others who are not presently living at peace with each other. The beauty of the Abrahamic faiths, of which Christianity is one, can be summed up this way: "Even with all our differences we draw from an ancient past as we build our shared global future."[6]

Before we delve into the main body of this book, allow me to provide a little background information about my life as a professional bassist in the music genre called Funk. In 2019 *The New York Times* featured a lengthy articled titled "The Glorious Return of Funk."[7] It chronicled how this musical genre, the very one that I helped to popularize, had once again taken center stage in American popular culture. *The Cambridge Dictionary* defines a curriculum vitae as "a short written description of your education, qualifications, previous jobs, and sometimes also your personal interests, which you send to an employer when you are trying to get a job."[8] What you are about to read is my CV as a Funk musician and social ethicist. The

4. Paris, *Spirituality of African Peoples*, 21.

5. Latin-dictionary.net, "Ligo," line 1.

6. MyJewishlearning.com, "This is Unity," para. 7.

7. Sloan, "Glorious Return," line 1.

8. Dictionary.cambridge.net, "Curriculum Vitae," para.1.

position I am applying for is one of guide. I want to be your guide through the complex and tangled web of hostility and distrust that race relations have become. However, before we embark on that journey, allow me to qualify myself as an expert in Funknology.

EDUCATION

BA Degree a.k.a. [James] Brown Association Degree

Meeting James Brown: Several years ago I was performing at a nightclub in Fresno, California, with a great band whose name I have forgotten. However, I do remember the band members' names: Tony Bartlett was on drums, "Baby" John Parrish on trumpet, Clark Baldwin on tenor saxophone, Janis Joplin's future bandleader Snooky Flowers on baritone saxophone, and there was a guitarist that my brother Bill had recommended, named Bobby Roach. Bobby was a good guitarist, but what really stood out about him was that he had played on many of Funk pioneer James Brown's early hits. At the time James Brown was called "the Godfather of Soul," and if you were to rank the influence that any one entertainer had on soul music, James Brown would have been at the top. However, the Godfather of Soul moniker was incomplete. That is because in reality, James Brown was also the Father of Funk as we know it today. Here is a glimpse into my initial classroom exposure.

James was scheduled to perform at the Fresno Fairgrounds and Bobby graciously invited Clark and myself to meet James Brown. Mr. Brown was generously listed at five foot six but in my eyes he was larger than life. James was more impressive to me than any athlete, celebrity, or politician that I could think of, including the president of the United States. In fact, the only human being walking the planet I admired more than James Brown was another Funk musician named Ray Charles.

James Brown's band had a reputation for performing his music flawlessly, mainly due to his perfectionistic leadership style. James may have been an obsessively driven band leader, but he also had a passion for the pursuit of civil rights for Black people. He was also known as "the hardest working man in show business," and that carried over to his fight for social justice. That makes it easy to see that Funk may have been birthed as a musical genre, but it would soon sprout wings and elevate to a much more prominent place at the very top of what was influencing Black culture in

America. It is worth stating that in black culture, "music is the language of the heart and the color of the soul," and Funk is Blackness personified.

Master of Bass Degree San Francisco U.

Leon's Creation: My brother and I accepted a long-term engagement at a nightclub in Anchorage, Alaska. While there I met a singer from Indiana named Gene Redding and we became friends. Gene often spoke of a monster guitarist named Jimmy McGhee, who lived in Ohio. He said that he thought Jimmy and I would "be something" together. When our engagement in Anchorage ended I contacted Gene and he in turn connected me with Jimmy. Gene was right because Jimmy and I complemented each other musically, and we later toured and recorded as Gene Redding and Funk.

Other musical opportunities would come out of my relationship with Gene and Jimmy, which consisted of playing bass behind blues singers Etta James and Lou Rawls, in addition to brief stints with the Four Tops and Wilson Pickett. Gene and Jimmy would eventually make their way to the San Francisco Bay Area where I was staying and we tried to form a band. Finances were tight, and Gene moved on to Los Angeles and Jimmy went back to the east coast. I joined a band named the 6/8 Paradox and we played at a teenage nightclub in Redwood City, California called the Winchester Cathedral. There was a band that was just starting out named Sly and the Family Stone that would occasionally follow our set. They would perform "after hours," which meant after most of the other clubs had closed.

Sly's band soon earned a recording contract with Columbia Records and would discontinue their rotation at the Winchester Cathedral. The club owner decided to invite another popular San Francisco band named the V.I.P.s to audition in hopes of finding a replacement for the Family Stone. They proved up to the task and were scheduled to have their own slot at the club. Unfortunately the club burned down before they ever had the chance to play one note. Following the blaze at the cathedral I bounced around with various bands, mostly with my close friend, guitarist Jerry Perez. Another trio of longtime friends named Lenny Goldsmith, Jerry Peterson, and Barry Frost had been playing in Denver during this time. When they returned to the Bay Area they had something that was really good going and I would soon join their band. About a year later I found myself in need of a new situation, and as fate would have it, I wound up in a brand new band with two of the members from the V.I.P.s, and that band became Leon's Creation.

Leon's Creation recorded one album in a mind-expanding style of Funk that was all about *soul*. For us Funk and soul were interchangeable concepts. The intent of our music could best be described as something similar in function to that of the human soul that author Wayne Dosick spoke of in this way: "That which makes . . . a person capable of thinking, knowing, reasoning and remembering . . . doing justly and feeling compassion—is the soul."[9] Justice and compassion were major components of the hippie ethos that we embraced wholeheartedly as a band. As to the music itself, this review from a website named "Funk My Soul" will give you some idea what we sounded like:

> A stomping set of Sly & The Family Stone-styled psyche-soul jams packed with brass, acid-rock guitar and coupla breaks . . . "In The Beginning" got a private pressing in 1969 and never saw a proper release. This San Francisco outfit . . . deserved better, 'cos on this evidence they really had something, easily the match of Tower Of Power, Buddy Miles or Ides Of March etc. etc. operating in a similar field at the time.[10]

Leon's Creation parlayed the "stomping set of . . . psyche-soul jams" into a regional hit with title track "This is the Beginning." Once that song began receiving a significant amount of airplay on local radio stations we were approached by David Kapralik and Stoneflower Productions, Sly Stone's and David's company. Shortly after signing with them the band was booked at an upscale nightclub on Broadway Street in San Francisco called Basin Street West. That performance would turn out to be a night to remember in more ways than one. A band from the east coast that was unknown to us was scheduled to be the other band on the bill. That band was George Clinton and the Funkadelic.

I have no way of knowing whether Sly was aware of the Funkadelic or not, but he did attend our gig that night for what would become a night when raw psychedelic Funk was on full display. That is because three out of the handful of bands in the world playing that style of music were in the same place at the same time, Sly Stone, George Clinton, and Leon's Creation. Or as George would later refer to the grouping in his memoir,

---

9. Dosick, *Living Judaism*, 2.
10. Funkmysoul.gr, "Leon's Creation," para. 3.

"a PaliafunkadelicmentLeon's Thing."[11] What was equally amazing is that none of us knew at the time that in a very short while we would be playing on each other's records in addition to doing live shows together.

Doctorate in Funknology

Dissertation supervisor Doctor John: One of the stops on my musical journey was to record and tour with the piano legend Dr. John. Dr. John's Funk was a blend of the rollicking piano style of Professor Longhair, who was cited by Tony Bolden as being the "originator of Funk and Rock and Roll,"[12] with Afro-Cuban rhythms—and a dash of New Orleans voodoo thrown in. That "rhumba-boogie Funk,"[13] as Atlantic Records executive Jerry Wexler would affectionately refer to it, would morph into a form of retro-Funk on an album I played on appropriately titled *Gumbo*.

That famous stew has been defined as, "a soup popular in the U.S. state of Louisiana, and is the official state cuisine. Gumbo consists primarily of a strongly-flavored stock, meat or shellfish, a thickener, and what Louisianans call the 'Holy Trinity' of vegetables, namely celery, bell peppers, and onions."[14] Ah yes, a tasteful blend is an accurate description of what happened when Dr. John's New Orleans piano met my San Francisco'd funky bass. The title for this book was birthed during this period of study. The *Gumbo* album has been one of Dr. John's most popular records over the decades, and *Rolling Stone* magazine once ranked it number 404 on its list of the 500 greatest albums of all time.[15]

Post-Doctoral Fellowship

Taken under the tutelage of George Clinton, the curator of Funk, and the mastermind of the Parliament-Funkadelic: Funk can be a descriptive term for the lived experience of people of African descent throughout the western diaspora and no one used that term better than George. For example, his *Chocolate City* was an album with an overt pro-Black theme. Being that

11. Clinton and Greenman, *George*, 136.
12. Bolden, *Funk*, 213.
13. Rebennack and Rummel, *Under a Hoodoo Moon*, 183.
14. Wikipedia.org, "Gumbo," para. 1.
15. Rollingstone.com, "500 Greatest Albums," para. 47.

African people were brought to US soil by force and not granted citizenship for hundreds of years—then denied civil rights after citizenship was granted—people of African descent were without a land of their own or a history of their own. George's vision for the creation of a chocolate city on American soil would be a reversal of all that.

I was a member of Rare Earth at the time and we would open shows for Parliament when they had a major hit titled "Give up the Funk." You can take my eyewitness account as gospel, what I observed during their show was a Black celebration of life in every meaning of the word. Funk provided hope for people of African descent that were able to survive in a country whose foundational documents excluded them, and whose subsequent policies were created to oppress them. Funk, as Ira Berlin wrote about the mid-Atlantic transport of slaves, provided "the will of the black people to survive, the determination not to be dehumanized by dehumanizing circumstances."[16] More on that later, but for now let us look at the positive psychological benefits that came with the funk. The last line from the Funkadelic song, "One Nation Under a Groove," summed up the optimism that funk instilled in Black people this way: "We are one nation on the move and nothin' can stop us now!" Or couched in more biblical terms, "The funk will inherit the earth."

Area of Research

It is difficult to discuss the funk without you having at least a basic understanding of the etymology of the word. Let us begin by looking at some definitions for the word as it will appear throughout these pages. Funk is about music, but funk is also about beauty. Funk is about the rhythms of life. Funk is also about struggle and the harsh realities that racial tensions have produced in the lives of millions. Funk is about all of that and more. For example, author Ricky Vincent said, "Funk is *funkiness,* a natural release of the essence within . . . Funk is at the extreme of everything."[17] And author David Thompson wrote, "Funk is the sound of the absolute organic purity that existed before there were words to mold the moment and it will be here long after it is gone," because *"Funk is human instinct!"*[18] I would add that funk is at its best when it is raw and real. It is the "real" aspect of

16. Berlin, *Making of African America,* 14.

17. Vincent, *Funk,* 3.

18. Thompson, *Funk,* vii.

funk that has been missing in our conversations on race. Frankly, we need to be more honest with each about what we really think about race and how we live as a result, and that is the funk of it.

WHAT IS THE FUNK?

To avoid any possible confusion I will capitalize the F when speaking of Funk as music and the resultant cultural world view. I will use a lowercase f when referring to funk as a state of mind of African peoples in the diaspora. I will also be *applying* (not defining) the word *Funk* in a variety of ways throughout this book. For now I want to hone in on one pertinent definition which says it "means, 'stinky' or 'musty smelling,' from the French funkière, 'smoke.'"[19] In a prior book I made reference to one way to compliment great Funk music is by using this phrase, "That's funkier than a gorilla's armpit."[20] If you can somehow bring yourself to imagine that particular aroma or scent—then you can imagine how bad the racism smells that Black people have had fanned in the direction of our figurative nostrils.

As you read this book please keep these words from Ian Haney Lopez's book *White by Law* close at hand, "Race matters . . . To be born black is to know an unchangeable fact about oneself that matters every day."[21] And it should be axiomatic that the same holds true for whites. It does matter to many whites when they come in contact with an unfamiliar (to them) Black person. Take a moment to reflect on this quote, "With slavery, blackness became stigmatized as servile and worse, and whiteness became a privileged condition made visible by its never-ending efforts to distinguish itself from blackness."[22] Said another way, European American identity is wrapped up in their whiteness, whereas African American identity is burdened by their Blackness.

The suffix *ology* is defined the following way in *The Oxford Dictionary*: "A subject of study; a branch of knowledge."[23] The letter *n* is frequently used as an abbreviation for the word *and*. I have shortened what would need to be a compound phrase to articulate the nouns *Funk* and *study* (ology) to one simple word, *Funknology*. Funknology then is the study of the rhythms of

19. Vocabulary.com, "Funk," para. 1.
20. Calhoun, *Art of God*, 54.
21. Lopez, *White by Law*, 21.
22. Brodkin, *How Jews Became White Folks*, 70.
23. Lexico.com, "Ology," line 1.

life as a socio-theological philosophy in a racial context. Funknology as an application is the synthesis of concepts drawn from art (sensory), science (intellectual), and the spirituality of being, which focuses on our relationship to and with the source of life, God.

It should be clear to you by now that this book is about more than Funk in the musical sense. As Cornel West has said, "This Funk is neither a skill nor an idea, not a world-view or a stance. Rather it is an existential capacity to get in touch with forms of kinetic orality . . . owing to the socialization in the patterns of Afro-American ways of *life* and *struggle*"[24] [Italics mine]. However, in spite of the struggles that African Americans continue to face, I can state without hesitation that Funk is a celebration of life in the midst of those struggles.

TOWARDS A FUNKNOLOGY OF HOPE

Yes, racism *has* produced lives of struggle for most Black and Native people in comparison with their white fellow-countrymen. That is the truth of it, and that is the Funk of it. It is also a condition this book was written to help change. There is an additional definition for the word *Funk* that can be found in *The Cambridge Dictionary*: "the state of being unhappy and without hope."[25] Henry Allen of *The Washington Post* once commented, "Funk once meant a shameful condition shunned by millions, a quality linked to aging bedclothes, depression, various low-rent odors and incapacitating fear."[26] Those are the general descriptions of the existence that millions of people of African and Native descent lived [and died] believing that was "simply life."

In one of my earlier books, I wrote that there have been white people in every generation who believed that race relations were just about right and only needed a minor tweak here and there to resolve any issues. There has also been a smaller number who have viewed any racial progress as being too much too soon and resisted it. That was true then and it is true now. However, there really are substantial problems related to race and they need addressing regardless of the inconvenience and at whatever the cost.

We could all learn something from John Hume, who spearheaded peace in Northern Ireland during an extremely violent time. He "argued

24. West, *Cornel West Reader*, 479.
25. Dictionary.cambridge.net, "Funk," para. 2.
26. Napier, *African American Literary Theory*, 98.

that the problem was less a physical border in Ireland, and more the division in people's minds. He long argued against 'binary identities' of British or Irish and for 'multiple identities' which could be held and celebrated alongside each other."[27] Perhaps one possible solution for us to consider can be found in these words used in a South African church service, "We believed it was right to withstand one another; now we are reconciled to understand one another."[28]

I write books with the hope of changing attitudes because in my view they are the root of the problem. That is because, unlike an isolated example of racist behavior, people's attitudes are deeply embedded and remain constant unless an effort is made to redirect them. They run the gamut of human emotion, and all of them influence the way people understand race and racism. That confluence of various types of emotion is what ultimately leads to the racist behavior this book addresses. In the United States attitudes about race range from ambivalent to passionate, from indifferent to obsessed, and on down the line. Gently confronting all of those attitudes in some way is one motivation behind this book. The desired outcome for my writing is summed up in this quote from Professor Jerry Root, "Every age needs an infusion of hope, a willingness to envision for succeeding generations the possibility that some degree of good can be achieved by every individual and every human endeavor."[29] All it takes for that to become reality is the right attitude and that can be acquired through this course in Funknology. Let's go!

27. Spiked-online, "John Hume," para. 4.
28. Tutu, *African Prayer*, 40.
29. Habl and Root, *On Being Human*, vii.

1

FLASHPOINTS—A PRELUDE

This chapter is a prelude to the three movements that comprise Funknology. I will refer to *flashpoints* in this chapter. One dictionary defines a flashpoint as "a place, event, or time at which trouble, such as violence or anger, flares up."[1] The layout of this book is similar to an orchestral suite in that it is structured around three thematically linked sections. The first is dedicated to Art, which is sensory and involves sight, sound, and the body. The second section looks at Science, which is more cerebral in nature and focuses on what it is we think about race, how we behave towards others, and how we live together because of those beliefs. The third section is named Being, which addresses the spiritual aspect of our shared humanity. Before we dive into Art, Science, and Being, I ask that you enter into a process of what I am calling "reverse deduction." That entails rethinking some of your present convictions about race by reanalyzing some incidents from the past.

The events you are about to read occurred as a direct result of America's ongoing incoherent social and legal policies concerning people of African descent. What follows contains only a small number of the lowlights from the historical record as it relates to race. The word *fragile* was recently inserted into the conversation on race in a popular book titled *White Fragility*. Author Robin DiAngelo defined white fragility as "the inability of white people to tolerate racial stress . . . and being indignant and defensive when confronted with racial inequality and injustice"[2]—effectively putting a limit on which grievances can be voiced by Black people.

1. Lexico.com, "Flashpoint," line 1.
2. Iqbal, "Interview," para. 5.

This is the fourth book I have written in an effort to gently move the conversation on race forward. My first book, *A Story of Rhythm and Grace,* contained my observations about the racial divide through the eyes of a black pastor working in predominantly white churches. My second, *The Art of God,* covered race and disability through the eyes of an artist, and we will revisit that coupling in the chapter titled "Aesthetics." My third book, *The Sounds of Love and Grace,* challenged the church about its poor race relations on ethical grounds. In none of my prior books did I express how *I felt,* only what *I saw,* for the reasons Ms. DiAngelo cited. In this book I will attempt to express a small number of my personal feelings in what is called "The Funk of It" at the end of each chapter.

Now a question for you. What would happen were we to use the word *fragility* in combination with Black instead of white? Let us begin our quest for an answer with this definition for *fragility* from *The Cambridge Dictionary*: "the quality of being easily damaged or broken."[3] Place the word *Black* in the front of that definition and form a sentence. It would read something like this: Black fragility is the quality of being easily damaged or broken—due to a long history of external social pressures. The type of fragility just mentioned is not referring to any inherent weakness in the make-up of Black people because our history tells a very different story. The African's story in America is one of strength, endurance, and survival in an environment polluted by racial oppression.

Gallup polling sums up what I am alluding to: "In America's fragile communities, residents face numerous barriers to opportunity that hinder their ability to lead fulfilling and prosperous lives."[4] I contend that the human psyche is incapable of restraining all of the frustration that persistent injustice and limited opportunity creates for an indefinite period of time. Sooner or later those internal frustrations make their way to the top, and as with a volcano, an eruption occurs. Those periodic eruptions are *flashpoints.* I have purposely used large sections of actual news accounts rather than my own summarizations because I did not want any perceived author bias to have an impact on the way you interpret these accounts.

We begin in the past because it is extremely difficult to approach the topics of race or racism without at least some understanding of the history related to the way racialized ideologies have been applied. The past is made up of very different stories for white people in contrast to other

3. Dictionary.cambridge.net, "Fragility," line 13.
4. Gallup, "Research Finds Fragile Community," line 1.

people of color. For example, most of what we know about the history of African interaction with Europeans is from histories written by the slave traders, consumers of slave labor, the apathetic, and possibly some who were intentionally misinformed. In any case, they can be histories that rely on many different sources, but unfortunately, as Zora Hurston observed, there is "not one word from the sold,"[5] meaning the Blacks themselves. The correctness of that history then becomes an epistemological one, and not a political or sociological one. Put simply, it is a matter of whose version of facts are to be used.

Race is still an extremely difficult topic and one that many would rather not discuss while others fail to see the need. To compound that, some of the examples you are about to read will be very hard to accept as actually happening to innocent human beings. That said, I would ask that you read these *flashpoints* as the lived experiences of real people and not just as horror stories in a film. I also ask that you try to place yourself in the shoes of those who made the decision to take the only action available to them in the face of so much suffering. It is difficult for most white Americans today to place themselves in that history. If that is you, please understand that these events are very much a part of *my* history. It has been said that "all histories are made by strong persons,"[6] and as you are about to see, the history of the African in America is really no different. As you read these *flashpoints*, please remember that this book was not written to make anyone feel guilt or discomfort. It was written to help all of us feel hopeful, but that will only come about if we honestly admit we have a problem.

NEW YORK CITY SLAVE REBELLION 1712— FLASHPOINT—AFRICAN ENSLAVEMENT

Take note of the date of this incident. It is 1712, right? Now look at the word *rebellion* that appears in the sentence before the date. What imagery comes to mind when you think of the word *rebellion*? Maybe the US Civil War. Maybe a set of unruly college students tearing up their hotel room on spring break. Let us put those images on hold for a moment and look at one dictionary's definition for rebellion: "an act of violent or open resistance to an established government or ruler."[7]

5. Walker and Hurston, *Barracoon*, 4.

6. Oz and Oz-Salzbeger, *Jews and Words*, 50.

7. Google.com, "Rebellion," line 1.

Can you now see at least two immediate problems with the subhead, which actually duplicates a newspaper headline from the time? One, who are the people doing the rebelling, and against what "established government or ruler" are they rebelling? If the first answer that your gut is giving you is, "Why, the American government," don't go there because it didn't exist. If "the slave owners" crossed your mind, your second question should be, "how is it that they came to be the owners of human beings, and who was it that granted them the right to rule over them?" What is really going on here is the establishment and reinforcement of a social construct through an immoral use of power that we have yet to deconstruct. Now to the facts.

Gabe Pressman recorded the facts of the event this way: "On the evening of April 6, the spark caught fire. That night, a group of approximately 23 slaves gathered in an orchard on Maiden Lane in the center of town. Armed with swords, knives, hatchets and guns, the group sought to inspire the city's slaves to rise up against their masters by staging a dramatic revolt."[8] Robert Hunter, the colonial governor of New York, later wrote of the revolt in a report designed to shed more light on why the event happened. "I must now give your Lordships an account of a bloody conspiracy of some of the slaves of this place, to destroy as many of the inhabitants as they could . . . when they had resolved to revenge themselves, for some hard usage they apprehended to have received from their masters."[9] Usage? What follows is the white response to what could only be described as a fight to procure for Blacks the right to exercise the natural human inclination toward freedom.

> Of the approximately 40 slaves brought to trial, 18 were acquitted and a few others were pardoned. The rest were brutally executed: four were burned alive; one was crushed by a wheel; one was kept in chains until he starved to death; a pregnant woman was kept alive until she gave birth and was then executed; and the others were hanged. In response to that slave rebellion, strict codes were enacted, which included—but were not limited to—harsher punishments as the slaveholders saw fit, decreased contact among slaves, and the prohibition of slave-owned firearms.[10]

If we were to accept the narrative that America was founded on Christian principles as accurate, then these punishments were carried out by

8. Lewis, "Slave Revolt," para. 5.

9. Hunter, "Governor reports on 1712 slave revolt," para 2.

10. Britannica.com, "New York slave rebellion," para. 3.

14

mainly Christians. I find it difficult to identify with people of faith who are willing to gloss over acts of violence towards other human beings by simply saying, "That was unthinkable, but that is just the way it was." Perhaps we should step back and take a moment to examine how we see the less powerful being treated right now. Is it possible that some of us are engaged in tomorrow's "unthinkable" without giving it much thought, just as those in the past were able to?

THE STONO REVOLT—FLASHPOINT—AFRICAN ENSLAVEMENT

One Sunday in 1739 the largest slave revolt in the history of the British colonies ended with the death of sixty people. Led "by an Angolan named Jemmy, a band of twenty slaves organized a rebellion on the banks of the Stono River. After breaking into Hutchinson's store the band, now armed with guns, called for their liberty . . . The band reached the Edisto River where white colonists descended upon them, killing most of the rebels."[11] What follows are the actual words that one freedom fighter said to his "army" following the battle, "He say: We don't lak slavery. We start to jine de Spanish in Florida. We surrender but we not whipped yet and we is not converted [to Protestantism]."[12] The soldier referred to a Spanish settlement near St. Augustine, Florida, named Fort Mose—which became the first "free Black" settlement—or the first chocolate city, in America.

Author Gerald Horne writes, "The Stono uprising struck terror in the minds of settlers, solidifying the perception that though enslaved Africans are necessary for development, their presence was dangerous and, therefore, they must be even more brutally oppressed."[13] Notice how easy it was for brutality to be accepted as the most effective "weapon" for use in controlling darker-skinned human beings. The specter of dangerous Blacks interrupting the social order was *the* justification for the suggestion that more violence was needed. Historian Peter Watson observed that "human beings have a large (and largely unconscious) group of rapid, intuitive biases in our everyday actions."[14] Are there people today that see violence towards darker-skinned people as still being the best option to control them?

11. Sutherland, "Stono Rebellion," para.1.

12. Nationalhumanitiescenter.org, "Stono Slave Rebellion," para. 18.

13. Horne, *Counter-Revolution of 1776*, 112.

14. Watson, *Convergence*, 345.

DEMERARA RIOTS 1823—FLASHPOINT—THE WHIP

Early in the nineteenth century, the colonial secretary of the British colony of Jamaica "ordered a ban of the flogging of enslaved women . . . and prohibited the use of the cart whip to goad reluctant slaves."[15] Whipping or beating was the method of choice for maintaining control. Its cruelty did not seem to bother very many in the white community at that time. In September of 1844, the *St. Louis Republican* reported that an eight-year-old Black girl had been whipped to death, with "The flesh on the back and limbs beaten to a jelly—one shoulder [bone] laid bare,"[16] and the perpetrators were acquitted. That is why when the whip was banned in Jamaica it suggested to many that freedom was at hand. However, nothing was further from the truth. The Africans were expected to perform like good slaves should. When the slaves "rebelled" and "rioted," what followed was that "at least a hundred were killed, fifty more executed, and others sentenced to 1,000 lashes—tantamount to a death sentence in itself."[17]

The Demerara riots are important to note because, rather than evoking sympathy in the minds and hearts of British politicians, "Opinions in Parliament hardened against any form of abolition [of slavery]."[18] The British Parliament saw the slaves' behavior as the problem, and they rejected the idea of any further relief for them. I have observed a similar attitude by some at the prospect of abolishing some of the violence on our city streets today. The victims are the problem. Sadly, that is the attitude of more Christians than I would have believed possible prior to the riots of 2020. There are many Christians that are more upset with the people pushing back against their treatment, than the racism that caused the unrest in the first place. It is shocking how much violence against another human being people are willing to condone, and even justify, if it is presented to them as being "necessary."

HOUSTON RIOTS 1917—FLASHPOINT—POLICING

"The Houston Riot of 1917," or "the Camp Logan Riot," were labels given by the media to describe the same event. The riots occurred when "soldiers

15. Cook, *Macaulay*, 132.
16. Simkin, "Whipping of a Slave," para. 18.
17. Cook, *Macaulay*, 132.
18. Cook, *Macaulay*, 132.

of the all-black 3rd Battalion, 24th Infantry—a unit of the famed Buffalo Soldiers"[19] rioted or committed mutiny. The *flashpoint* appeared to be an incident involving a police officer who pistol whipped a man for "insubordination" and "supposedly said, 'That's the way we do things in the South. We're running things, not the damned niggers.'"[20] That last statement reflects the attitude some people have when people of color confront them about racism: "We're running things," and then they close their ears and their minds.

If the hearsay piece of the previous quotes raise any question in your mind, "An Army report confirmed the Houstonians view of black soldiers, concluding that both police and white citizens felt that 'a nigger is a nigger and that his status is not affected by the uniform he wears.'"[21] As many believe to be the case today, "'This was a problem created by community policing in a hostile environment' says Paul Matthews, founder of Houston's Buffalo Soldiers National Museum, which examines the role of African-American soldiers during US military history . . . 'The soldiers were standing up for America when it wasn't standing up for them.'"[22]

EMMETT TILL—FLASHPOINT—MURDER— PROTECTING WHITENESS IN 1956

This is a bare-bones account of what happened to this young man:

> Emmett Till, a 14-year-old African-American boy, was murdered in August 1955 in a racist attack that shocked the nation and provided a catalyst for the emerging civil rights movement . . . Till was visiting relatives in Money, Mississippi, when he was accused of harassing a local white woman . . . Relatives of the woman abducted Till, brutally beating and killing him before disposing of his body in a nearby river.[23]

Why did this child's murder happen? The short answer lies within the fact that for some, there was nothing held in higher esteem than white womanhood. A Black male could be whipped and/or killed for merely

---

19. Pvamu.edu, "1917 Houston riots," para 2.
20. Pvamu.edu, "1917 Houston riots," para. 18.
21. Pvamu.edu, "1917 Houston riots," para. 14.
22. Jeffrey, "Remembering the black soldiers," para.19.
23. History.com.editors, "Emmett Till," line 1.

looking at a white woman in public. Emmett Till, accused of disrespect toward a white woman, was beaten beyond recognition, his eyes removed, his tongue cut out, and castrated. I watched a video of the funeral and the attenders' reaction to the child's mutilated body inside the open casket were consistent: horrified! One attendee referred to what he had just seen as the most heinous and barbaric treatment of a child in the history of mankind. Why this amount of brutality was foisted upon a fourteen-year-old is incomprehensible to me.

Now let us look at how the wheels of "justice" ground to a halt for the family and friends of Emmett Till. Till's murderers—a Mr. Bryant, and a Mr. Milam—were charged with Till's kidnapping and murder. Then for some reason, it only took one hour of deliberation for an all-white jury to return a verdict of not guilty. To make matters worse, one year later, the duo admitted to murdering Till in an interview with a national magazine, *Look*. And they were proud of it! It is not just the loss of life that angers people in the Black community. It is the fact that there has not always been a price to pay for those who have taken their loved ones away. Much of the media focuses on the deceased following a shooting tragedy, but it affects a much larger group of family and friends than the names in the headlines. There is so much unnecessary grief. And finding a justification that satisfies one group of people does not soothe the hurt of another. Emmett Till's mother demanded an open casket to force America to see the outcome of racism and maybe we need to be willing to look at it today.

BULL CONNOR—FLASHPOINT—POLICE BRUTALITY

The name Bull Connor was a symbol of a time when police brutality was televised on the nightly news. The images I saw on television as a kid were of Black people's arms flailing away attempting to protect themselves from powerful streams of water gushing from firehoses originally designed to preserve life and property. Police dogs were arbitrarily biting the closest person that they could find. Children, women, and men were all equal opportunity targets.

The civil rights movement had ushered in a new era of violence against Blacks, and because of television, the ugliness would reach the eyes of a nation. I will not attempt to describe the horrific scenes that I witnessed as a child because frankly, they still hurt! Instead, I want to do something different from what books typically do. I want to provide you with a YouTube link to a thirty-second clip and ask that you to take a few seconds to go online line and see exactly what I witnessed. Here is the link: https://www.youtube.com/watch?v=hPrHwmiUMHo. One PBS article had this to say about Bull Connor, the man who orchestrated that violence:

> Eugene "Bull" Connor was Birmingham's Commissioner of Public Safety in 1961 when the Freedom Riders came to town. He was known as an ultra-segregationist with close ties to the KKK. Connor encouraged the violence that met the CORE Freedom Riders at the Birmingham Trailways bus station by promising local Klansmen that, "He would see to it that 15 or 20 minutes would elapse before the police arrived." In 1962 he sought the Democratic gubernatorial nomination, beginning his campaign in January by promising to buy one hundred new police dogs for use in the event of more Freedom Rides.[24]

What needs to be fully understood here, and as hard as it might be to fathom, is that racist attitudes were not considered abnormal or even bad not that long ago. To act on them was more like bad manners than poor character. White people were free to use the "N word" in public, ridicule all aspects of Black culture for sport, and do it right in front of us. Those of us who did not appreciate that type of treatment and said something about it were characterized as "not knowing their place." If Black people voiced objections, then something was wrong with *them*.

Today as I watch politicians and Christians scrambling to try and find a "balanced" response to the protests of the unending stream of citizen's deaths at the hands of law enforcement, my biggest concern is the impact that the images of bodies on the street is having on the psyche of impressionable Black youth. Conservatives are calling for the perceived offenders to "behave better," and liberals are calling for police reform. The kids I just referred to are asking themselves, "Am I next?" Fear is not the best ingredient for a well-adjusted childhood. I know that Bull Connor negatively affected my life as a very young child. Maybe it is time we seriously consider what it is our children are watching us condone, and what we are willing to accept as normal. After all, they are our future.

24. Pbs.org, "Meet the players," para. 1.

THE BLACK PANTHERS—FLASHPOINT—POLICE
BRUTALITY

The Black Panther Party was formed in 1966. Their existence engendered fear and suspicion in the hearts of most of white America regardless of their political or religious stripe. In May of 1967, the Panthers garnered national attention by attending a session of the California legislature with loaded rifles. Images of heavily armed young Black men inside the walls of a government building were televised in the homes of white families all across America.

The Panthers' objective was to send a message to the authorities that they would no longer tolerate the police brutality that had become so common in the Black section of Oakland, California. However, the vast majority of whites interpreted the show of force as proof of the militancy, and the "belligerence" of Black youth culture, and they were terrified. It was not long after the Party gained notoriety that my older brother Bill became involved. What follows was excerpted from a New York radio program:

> Emory Douglas, the Black Panther Party's Minister of Culture, heard Bill Calhoun and his friends singing harmony, [and] he had an idea: a revolutionary black power singing group, complete with dance routines and costumes . . . The band was called the Lumpen, from Karl Marx's *lumpenproletariat*. That may be the least funky band name ever, but Calhoun knew how to put on a show. As bandleader Billy King, he had been gigging up and down California. He had a regular show at a club in San Francisco when the Watts riots and smaller Bay Area uprisings broke out. "The reaction of the club owner," Calhoun recalled, "when he started talking about 'them niggers'—it hit me that, yes I am Billy [Calhoun] . . . but I'm also one of 'them niggers.' That changed things for me."[25]

What follows is a sample of Black Panther Party Funk in the form of lyrics written by my brother.

> There were times,
> We stood by,
> like we could not see,
> But, there won't be no more,
> Won't be no more.
> We'll get guns, To defend our community,
> So there won't be no more

25. Wnyc.org, "All You Need," para. 2.

Can't be no more,
We'll control, Our destiny
No more murder of our people,
In their sleep,
To this way of life,
We're closing the door, So there won't be no more,
Won't be no more.

Notice that when guns were mentioned in the song, it was in a strictly defensive context. Was the perceived need for guns simply a civil rights era paranoia? Or was police brutality an actual lived reality for minority people in Oakland and beyond? Did the threat of police brutality subside with the end of the hippie and civil rights eras? Yes and no! After you read the next example of an all-too-familiar occurrence within the African American community, take a moment to reread the lyric to my brother's song, and focus in on the lyric "in their sleep."

BREONNA TAYLOR MARCH 13, 2020—FLASHPOINT —POLICE KILLING

Breonna Taylor and her boyfriend Kenneth Walker were asleep inside their apartment when they were awakened by knocks on the front door. What happened next was that Breonna was shot dead by Louisville, Kentucky police officers, "after they allegedly executed a search warrant of the wrong home . . . [They] used a battering ram to force open the green door with a gold No. 4 hanging on it, at which point police say they are met with a gunshot that strikes Mattingly in the thigh . . . The three officers blindly return fire with more than 25 bullets—some entering other apartments, including one with a 5-year-old child."[26]

The end result of this tragedy is that the Taylor family received a 12-million-dollar settlement, which was one of the largest ever paid in the United States in a case of police brutality and alleged police misconduct. The reason why the shooting was characterized as alleged misconduct was that "A subsequent police report contained errors including Ms. Taylor's injuries listed as 'none,' and saying no force was used to enter, when a battering ram was used."[27] Can you see why Black people could only scratch

---

26. Carrega and Ghebremedhi, "Inside the Investigation," para. 5.
27. Bbc.com, "Breonna Taylor," para. 7.

their heads in amazement when a decision was made by the local grand jury not to file charges against the officers involved?

GEORGE FLOYD KILLING—FLASHPOINT—POLICE BRUTALITY

A local news agency, the ABC affiliate in Minneapolis, reported "[George] Floyd, a black man in handcuffs, died on May 25 after [Derek] Chauvin, who is a white officer, pressed his knee against Floyd's neck as he said he couldn't breathe . . . Chauvin is charged with second-degree murder and other crimes; Thomas Lane, J. Kueng and Tou Thao are charged with aiding and abetting."[28] It was the killing of Mr. Floyd that ignited much of the unrest of the long, hot summer of 2020. This has resulted in a brighter spotlight being directed at the Black Lives Matters movement overall, and the professional athletes who believed protesting for racial justice to be part of their civic duty. I mention Black Lives Matters to point out that there are some who would deflect attention from the serious issue of unnecessary loss of life by focusing on the politics of the leadership of the group, overlooking the feelings of the families of those whose loved ones are prematurely in their graves.

Athletes protesting police activities began a few years before these recent incidents, when San Francisco quarterback Colin Kaepernick began to kneel during the playing of the national anthem. About "taking a knee" Kaepernick stated, "There's a lot of things that need to change. One specifically: police brutality. There's people being murdered unjustly and [others] not being held accountable. People are being given paid leave for killing people. That's not right. That's not right by anyone's standards."[29] He clearly stated that his protests were about police brutality, but many who saw how the protests were carried out did not hear him. One uneducated response came from fellow pro quarterback Drew Brees, who weighed in on the Black Lives Matter protests following the George Floyd killing this way:

> "I will never agree with anybody disrespecting the flag of the United States of America or our country," Brees said. "Let me just tell you what I see or what I feel when the national anthem is played, and when I look at the flag of the United States. I envision my two grandfathers, who fought for this country during World War II,

28. Abc7.com, "George Floyd," para. 3.
29. Biderman, "Colin Kaepernick," para. 4.

one in the Army and one in the Marine Corps. Both risking their lives to protect our country and to try to make our country and this world a better place."[30]

Columnist Geoffrey Norman wrote an op-ed piece under this banner: "What We Have Here Is Failure . . . to Miscommunicate."[31] His headline was a spoof on a famous line from the classic movie *Cool Hand Luke* where a prison boss said to the Paul Newman's convict character that the problem they were having was a failure to communicate, which ends with there being people you just can't reach. Did Colin Kaepernick fail to communicate, or did he "miscommunicate" perfectly that his protests were in response to dead bodies and not a flag? I think we must consider a third option. When the topic of race is center stage, some people simply can't be reached regardless of how well one communicates.

"ONE-EYED BLIND"

It is reasonable to assume that Mr. Brees would not be aware of the fact that there were many black grandparents fighting in those same wars who may have had different motivations for doing so. You see, a Black male in the 1940s could be drafted into the army of a country that forbade him from riding on buses, drinking from public water fountains, going to public beaches, and even walking on certain streets after dark. If he refused to fight because he believed that he had never been treated like a full citizen, he risked being shot as a traitor. Those grandparents were granted the right to die, but not the right to live. There are instances when the tracks of racial equality do not run parallel but crisscross. However, there really is no way for a person to know that unless they have actually made the journey themselves—and in matters of white/Black race issues, it is impossible to cross the tracks you are on to the other side without a considerable amount of effort.

In August of 2020, the commissioner of the National Football League, who is white, issued the following statement: "These are not people [kneeling players] who are unpatriotic. They're not disloyal. They're not against our military. In fact, many of those guys were in the military, and they're

---

30. Pickman, "Drew Brees."
31. Norman, "What We Have Here."

[from] a military family."[32] Those words appear to be remorse for the media's mischaracterizations that were allowed to linger in the minds of the general public for business reasons. Do you believe that morality and fairness should be subordinate to profit? Put another way, would you be willing to risk your financial security in order to right a wrong done to someone from a racial group different than your own?

RICHARD PRYOR—FLASHPOINT —POLICE BRUTALITY

The late great comedian Richard Pryor foresaw today's conversation about policing in a monologue he performed in the 1970s: "Cops put a hurting on your [black people's] a**, man, you know? They really degrade you. White folks don't believe cops degrade. Oh, come on. . . . I'm tired of this harassment of police officers."[33] Mr. Pryor's comic relief aside, the fact that he only needed to reference police brutality to elicit laughter suggests that its existence was a lived reality for a good percentage of his audience.

There are many people who are quick to write off every example of police violence as just an isolated incident regardless of the number or the frequency. Would not the fact that police brutality was broached in a comedy skit almost fifty years ago militate against "an unusual occurrence" being a satisfactory defense? What people who hold that view fail to understand about the way Black people are policed is this: whatever is happening now is a continuation of something that was happening *then*.

THE FUNK OF IT

The *flashpoints* we have just discussed are but a sampling in order to illustrate one important reality. Racial unrest has been a constant blight on the American self-image since the country's founding. Consider the wave of race riots that swept the nation's cities in 2020 and the mood they left the country in. Those horribly tragic events were not isolated, anomalous events. *New York Times* writer Virginia Postrel states, "From 1964 to 1971, there were more than 750 riots, killing 228 people and injuring 12,741

---

32. Espn.com, "Roger Goodell," para. 6.
33. McCluskey, *Richard Pryor*, 232.

others. After more than 15,000 separate incidents of arson, many black urban neighborhoods were in ruins."[34]

If our history had been one of a more loving people those examples would not exist. However, as tragic and inhumane as the *flashpoints* were that we just studied, we must remain optimistic that we can and will do better! Mark Twain gave us a gentle push in the direction we need to take in order to correct that when he said, "Loyalty to petrified opinion never yet broke a chain or freed a human soul."[35] Make no mistake about it, racist attitudes have ossified in the minds of so many Americans that changing is inconceivable to them. It is time to completely eliminate the scourge of racism because it stigmatizes its target from birth to death. It is going to take all of us to get that done but I believe that together we can. I long for the day when the human race reaches the understanding that when something happens to one of us, it has an effect on all of us.

34. Postrel, "Consequences," para.3.
35. Brainyquote.com, "Mark Twain."

Part One

THE ARTISTIC EYE

"The essential function of art is moral."
—D. H LAWRENCE

2

AESTHETICS

The great Swiss Reformer Ulrich Zwingli played the violin, flute, and harp. Because his interests spanned multiple disciplines there were some who refused to take him seriously. Even though he was a serious and influential theologian, one critic named Han Salat wrote, "Zwingli was practiced in puerilities and frivolities, taught drum-beating, playing the lute, the harp, and was a complete musical pedant."[1] Ouch! The fact that he was a monster musician led some to be suspicious of his religious zeal and theological knowledge. I mention this up front because throughout the remainder of this book I will be speaking to you as a Funk musician, which comes from my artistic side, and also as a pastor, which comes from my theological side. I ask that you let go of any internal tension the merging of those two aspects of my being might cause you. It is my position that the arts do not weaken one's theology. In fact, together theology and art can inspire the Christian imagination to, in the words of Amos Wilder, "meet the new dreams, mystiques, and mythologies that are gestating in our time."[2]

I have long had a deep love for the city of Amsterdam, dating back to when I played music at a large festival there several years ago. To this day I can picture everything about that gig. I remember that the architecture throughout the city was beautiful. The people were beautiful and the vibe at the concert was beautiful. I am aware that I may have overused the word *beautiful* and I may have violated a professional writer's rule in the process. I did this to demonstrate the many applications that word can lend itself to. Moreover, there are few words elastic enough to describe a person, a

1. Wilder, *Theopoetic*, 51.
2. Wilder, *Theopoetic*, 1.

building, and the music played at a concert attended by several thousand kids high on marijuana. There really is no limit to the number of ways the word *beautiful* can be used as a descriptor, and that is my point.

There is another word that might be just as elastic as the word *beautiful* and that is *art*. Frank Burch Brown offers two applications for it, saying, "There is a connection between artistic production and aesthetic appreciation."[3] The authors of *Art as Therapy* suggest a third application by saying that "art has a role in rebalancing us emotionally."[4] That last one may be true for a lot of people but it has certainly not been true for me. When my wife and I visited Amsterdam in 2017, Julaine, who is an art lover, "dragged" me from museum to museum to view world-renowned art. Being a complete art illiterate, I had no idea what I was looking at or why I should be impressed. The trip was wonderful, but my lack of art awareness made my time in the museum more an activity of loving my wife than one of loving art.

It was not until I began researching for this book that I learned why. I opened a book titled *Great Themes in Art* with the hope of educating myself about what it is other people are able to see when they find beauty in a work of art. I did not get the answers I was looking for, but at least my eyes were opened to some possible reasons why I was unable to see what others were seeing. The book was very helpful, but my big breakthrough came at a small group meeting one Sunday night. A friend who is a budding artist explained that he was learning how to mix three colors in a way that would give the illusion that the painting he was working on had depth to it. That meant his goal for the painting was to get people to perceive that there was depth to something that only existed on a completely flat surface.

Just like that, the cliché that says beauty is in the eyes of the beholder made much more sense. I learned that it was what I allowed my eyes to see that had been holding me back. I had been too much of a literalist. If I looked at a painting of a building, I saw a building, not the artist's interpretation of a building. My friend learned to manipulate colors in such a way that people perceived depth where none existed. People who appreciate art will someday stand in front of his painting and accept his illusion. Now that I have reconfigured my understanding about how to view art, I may be able to see depth too. Reaching that understanding also caused me to consider just how important acceptance is as it applies to other areas of life.

3. Brown, *Religious Aesthetics*, 78.
4. De Botton and Armstrong, *Art as Therapy*, 30.

At the museums in Amsterdam, the limited scope of my subjective lens had caused me to not accept the artists' renderings the way he or she had intended and so I missed out. I am not talking about a mistake in judgment here, but a complete ignorance about the quality of something. We have all had a similar experience. My ignorance about art harmed no one. However, to reject something without a full understanding of what it is you are looking at does great harm when it comes to race relations—and it happens every day.

BEAUTY IS ALL AROUND US

The opening sentences of the book *On Being Human* state, "Not without reason is the world called, in the Greek language, cosmos, that is, beautiful; and in the Latin, mundus, meaning pure. Everything in it is beautiful, pure, delightful and charming, and the visible beauty is painted by the invisible God."[5] The ancient Greek rendering of the word *cosmos* that the author used is similar to our word *adorn*. We use a form of that word to say something enhances the beauty of another object—think *cosmetologist*. That is what the arts do: they add beauty to life itself. Music makes you want to sing or dance. A book takes you to places you've never been. And the visual arts open your eyes to things you had not ever imagined. Gregory Wolfe suggests in his wonderful book *Beauty Will Save The World* that, "In a politicized age, constricted by the narrowness of ideology, few people really believe that art provides the necessary contemplative space that pulls us back from the world of action in order to send us back wiser and more fully human."[6]

At the same time, Nicholas Wolterstorff observes, "Works of art equip us for action. And the range of actions for which they equip us is very nearly as broad as the range of human action itself."[7] Allow me to break down that quote a tiny bit using a paraphrase of a P-Funk song, "art frees your mind so your [arse] can follow." Remember my liberal use of the word *beautiful* earlier? Let us do it again. In the introduction of the book *The Aesthetic Mind* the authors discuss the universality of aesthetics and they pose some interesting questions. "Is natural beauty for example not to be distinguished from moral beauty, which, again is to be further distinguished from artistic

5. Habl and Root, *On Being Human*, 1.
6. Wolfe, *Beauty*, 23.
7. Wolterstorff, *Art in Action*, 4.

31

beauty?"[8] Beauty is all around us and is capable of reaching deep down in our souls. Hopefully you are now better able to see the depth and breadth of the field of aesthetics. The question that should follow is what is aesthetics and why is it important?

Aesthetics is "a set of principles concerned with the nature and appreciation of beauty, especially in art."[9] In other words, aesthetics can be the judgment that is made about the beauty of an object through applying one's own subjective criteria. One way to reach those judgments can be found in the root word, "Aisthetika, which is the Greek word meaning . . . the things that we perceive through the senses."[10] And Frank Burch Brown informs us that *aesthetica* is not simply a matter of inherent beauty, but "all those things employing a medium in such a way that its perceptible form and 'felt' qualities become essential to what is appreciable and meaningful."[11] That is important because to live "aesthetically" is to orient our lives towards a proper response to all that is beautiful in the created order, and that includes everyone within it.

At a later point in this chapter we will replace the word *art* with *race* to keep our conversation consistent, but for now I want to change lanes and slip into the world of disability. In the book referenced earlier, *Great Themes in Art*, there is a full-page depiction of a bronze statue of what most certainly was the "ideal male" in the mind of the sculptor. The man is nude, which enables you to see his well-developed muscular build right down to his ripped stomach and bulging calf muscles. The sentence describing the photo says, "The beautifully balanced, proportioned, and toned body of a bronze figure of a Greek god, probably Zeus but perhaps Poseidon, embodies an ideal that has inspired many later generations,"[12] including our own.

BODY BEAUTIFUL

For many in Western society it is all about the body, and the ideal body at that. For instance, in 2019 "the U.S. weight loss market [was] now worth a record $72 billion."[13] And when it comes to spending on gym member-

8. Schellekens and Goldie, *Aesthetic Mind*, 3.

9. Lexico.com, "Aesthetics," line 1.

10. Hennigar, "Manipulate Aisthetika," line 2.

11. Brown, *Religious Aesthetics*, 100.

12. Walford, *Great Themes*, 59.

13. Prnewswire.com, "Weight Loss," line 1.

ships, the "market size of the global fitness and health club industry has been steadily increasing in recent years, exceeding 96 billion U.S. dollars in 2019."[14] For people living around the globe bodies are big business too. In addition to the enormous number of resources we put towards caring for and beautifying our bodies, the medical field spends more time and money researching ways to heal the body. Even with all of the focus directed at the human body, many do not see it as a spiritual component of our being, only the racial aspect of it.

BODIES

The Ideology of the Aesthetic begins, "Aesthetics is born out of a discourse of the body."[15] Let us turn a corner and move our discussion towards one about the disabled body and then the black body. I hope that when we are finished you will better understand the way that both sets of bodies have been perceived in the Western world, and that has been as less than equals. I have learned to see the beauty in bodies of people living with a disability, but as with art in Amsterdam, it did not come naturally to me. I want to share some of that process with you.

MOTHER BEAUTIFUL

I lost my mom several years ago. Her passing hit me very, very, hard. The unbearable sadness I felt the day of her funeral was not because we were close, it was because we were not close, at least physically. My rock and roll lifestyle was a stark contrast to her life, a life that had been dedicated to ministry since her early childhood in her father's church. That is the major reason why I had avoided her for so many years. I knew that if she had seen me in the condition I was in on a regular basis that she would have been heartbroken and uncomfortable on many levels.

She would have been uncomfortable because she would have had to watch me destroy myself knowing there was nothing she could do to "fix me." That is a tough place to be. We have all been there at one time or another concerning a loved one, haven't we? You look at someone's condition, your heart breaks for them, then the fact that you are powerless to change

14. Statista.com, "Health & Fitness," line 2.
15. Eagleton, *Ideology of The Aesthetic*, 13.

33

things for them sinks in, and it becomes difficult for you. At that point we often console ourselves with something along the lines of it is better for all parties to just stay away. That may or may not be true, but that is how I handled it, and I would wager I was not the first to do it. That said, since that time I have come to believe that avoiding people you can't fix is not always the best course of action, even if it makes you uncomfortable.

My mom's devout religious beliefs translated to how she actually lived her life. She held a Bible-centric world view of the first order. What I mean by that is she took what the Scriptures said to be more than religious advice; she believed the words on those pages were "true-truth." She believed the Bible was accurate and completely trustworthy. Occasionally she would speak of her mortality in an effort to prepare me for that eventual day when she would receive her heavenly reward. She drilled it into my head that on that day I should not view the body in the casket as her. She would cite these words from 2 Corinthians: "For we know that if the earthly tent we live in is destroyed, we have a building from God, an eternal house in heaven, not built by human hands"[16] to assure me that the real "Mom" was in a much better place.

But even with all the advance training and preparation I received from her, it did not prevent me from having an irresistible urge to kiss her that one last time, and I did. She had been right all along though, because that body in the casket was not her. Her body was still and cold but all throughout her life she had been vivacious and warm. A body was there, but she was alive in heaven, and very much alive in my heart. The place where I have put that valuable life lesson to use is in the disabled community, or the differently abled as I have come to affectionately call this wonderful group of people. Note that I called a people group with various degrees of "disfigurement" wonderful. I probably would not have chosen the word *wonderful* to describe my friends in the disabled community had I not stopped seeing a person as being identical with their bodies. Thanks again, Mom, for planting seeds in me that would bear fruit later in life.

BEAUTIFUL BODIES

I want to share with you the way my mom's use of Scripture went from being merely a theological concept to being actualized in my ministry. In two of my earlier books I told about how I came to be involved with the differently

16. 2 Cor 5:1, NIV.

abled community as a minister. I attributed it to meeting a woman named Sam and forming a relationship with her. I characterized meeting her as my "introduction" into that world. The story is absolutely true, but as with many truths, that story was not all of the truth.

Joyce

My first cousin on my dad's side, named Joyce, was what people used to call "retarded." We lived in San Jose, California and Joyce's family lived about seventy miles north in Pittsburgh, California. We would drive to visit them on weekends, and they would reciprocate and drive down to visit us. There was not a consistent pattern to those visits, they just seemed to happen. However, there was one thing that was consistent and that was my discomfort with having to be in the presence of one of my closest blood relatives. I am really ashamed to admit this today even though I was quite young. My hope for sharing this is that it might free you to examine your present attitude towards people that you run across who are in a similar condition. Maybe you need to admit to experiencing a degree of discomfort when you see someone who is living with what is often called an intellectual disability. It could very well be that admission is the first step towards a new perception of what is and is not beautiful. I wish that Joyce had been my first step in that direction but unfortunately there were many more missteps to come.

Jim

Today I realize that my attitude towards my relative stayed with me for a while and even got worse over time. Meet Jim Lewis. My mom was musical and belonged to a choral group named the San Jose Municipal Chorus, and a local music school named the San Jose Institute of Music, both founded by LeRoy V. Brant. There was also a male African American singer with a killer baritone voice that was a part of one or both. I need to say, having worked with the more famous singer Lou Rawls, who had a similar voice, Jim could hold his own with him any day. However, there was one area in which Lou and Jim differed: their bodies! Jim had no legs below the buttocks. Both of his arms did not have hands, although one of them had a very large phalange that looked like a very large finger, while the other "hand" had two smaller versions.

Later I learned what may have been his condition, Congenital Limb Deficiencies. This occurs when part of a limb is missing and/or other parts of the body have not formed normally. Dr. Douglas G. Smith wrote that in these cases, "limb loss is devastating both physically and emotionally."[17] And as it is with racism, those affected "are going through something that no one should have to go through."[18] Still, Jim had a profound effect on me in more than one way. While I was impressed by his enormous musical gift, I was equally repulsed by his body, and I would go to my room to hide whenever Mom had him over. He would "walk" in on two prosthetic legs as he supported his weight on crutches. Even the simple task of ambulating thirty or so yards from a car to our front door was a challenge for him. That is because having to negotiate crutches without having hands took time and effort. He was proud though, and didn't seem to want help.

Once inside, my parents would help him take off his legs and place him on a chair at the dinner table. For me, it went downhill from there. He wanted to feed himself and holding a fork consistently did not always happen. That meant there was often more food on him and on the table than what made its way to his mouth. I am ashamed to admit that my revulsion morphed into anger because I was being inconvenienced by his presence. I did not learn from that experience though, because in a few short years my terrible attitude toward people living with a disability would be on full display once again.

Rancho Linda

Rancho Linda School's Facebook page lists it as a residential center for special education, but when I was a teenager it was called Rancho Linda School for Retarded Children. Retarded was a name given to people with "mental disabilities," whether it was cognitive, a psychological disorder, or developmental disability. One year my older brother Bill took a job at the school as a counselor. True to his nature, he dove headfirst into his work and gave his all, which included bringing some of the students to our house for meals. That gave me the opportunity to repeat my stellar performances of interacting with those who would one day be said to have "special needs." In my mind they were not special, and they needed to stay away from me because they just made me feel weird. That was my attitude towards them

17. Smith, "Congenital," line 1.
18. Smith, "Congenital," line 2.

and I am ashamed to admit that most of the time I wished they would just disappear so that I would not have to see them.

JUDGED AND JURIED ART

I have served on the board of the Austin Interfaith Arts and Music Festival, whose mission it was to find commonalities between people of different ethnicities and faiths through the use of visual and performing arts by featuring juried artists. What is a juried artist? A juried work of art is one that has been presented before a panel of judges who determine the quality and value before it is deemed worthy to be presented at a particular art show. A juried artist is the creator or producer of that work. I may have had to learn what a juried visual artist was, but my experience has given me a sense of what it feels like to be a judged musical artist. I can assure you that the evaluations made by art and music critics alike are often very subjective in nature and often flat-out inaccurate.

Judgments of art, then, are always subjective. So how should artwork be judged if not through the observations of a qualified art critic? Should it be judged according to the number of strokes that each painter used on the work? How about the price each artist paid for the materials they used? Common sense would suggest that better quality materials would produce a better product, right? Aren't those exercises in circular logic similar to what we do when we use subjective observations to "qualify" racial groups by arbitrarily deciding their value and worth? Consider the criteria you use to determine the quality and value of another human being. The often used, "I don't," is really not an acceptable response because we all do. The only way progress can be made is if we are humble enough to admit it. However, my main point is just to make sure you are aware of what the methodology is that you are using.

Back to juried art. A gallery named the Salon, located in France, was, "for almost 150 years (c.1740–1890) . . . the most prestigious annual or biannual art event in the world."[19] It goes without saying that there was stiff competition among artists to have their work shown there, and the jurors were very particular about what would be allowed in. However, "The 1865 Salon accepted Olympia, a painting of a reclining nude glaring out at the viewer, but its reception was one of outrage. The public was aghast by the unflattering manner in which Manet painted her, the harsh lighting on her

19. Visual-arts-cork.com, "Paris Salon," para. 1.

pale, rough skin, and the fact that he [Manet] laid bare the fact that she was a prostitute awaiting her next client."[20]

How did they know she was a prostitute? They reached the conclusion by looking at her Black attendant. It seems that in every earlier era of Western culture the presence of a black or dark-skinned body signals low morality. So even artists cannot resist the temptation to use darkness to portray something sinister and undesirable. In a sense, then, bodies speak languages. And we all respond to different kinds of body language. As one article puts it, "Body language is a powerful indicator of others' emotions in social interactions, with positive signals triggering approach and negative ones retreat and defensiveness. Intergroup and interracial factors can influence these interactions."[21] So, the question should be, which type of signals am I receptive to? And the second question should be, what do I really believe about the differences between Black and white bodies?

GOD DOESN'T JUDGE DARK SKIN—HE JUDGES DARK HEARTS

Blackness has come to be synonymous with all that is negative. Many people are of the opinion that racism is not why young unarmed Black men are frequently killed by police, that our society's aversion to blackness in general is. Consider this quote from 2016, before the recent and intensified racial strife: "The roots of racist oppression lie in anti-blackness: the most abhorred side of colorism's spectrum."[22] Place the word *dark* before any noun and it becomes negative. Place the word *black* in front of a noun and the perceived negativity is intensified. Color psychology means that "black is often used as a symbol of menace or evil . . . It's used to represent treacherous characters such as Dracula and is often associated with witchcraft."[23] It is little wonder that so many artists use black as a symbol, because many painters believe that symbols should advance an emotion or idea. However, sometimes bad ideas result in bad consequences. Imagine what it would be like to spend your whole life in an environment where your body's appearance was used as a symbol for criminality and low morals. If you are unable to imagine that, then this recent dream of mine should help.

20. Blumberg, "Vile or Visionary," para. 3.
21. Watson and de Gelder, "How White and Black Bodies," para. 1.
22. Thu, "Anti-blackness," para. 9.
23. Supunsala, "Color Symbolism," para. 2.

One recent night I dreamed I was a Black medical doctor visiting a white couple who were also friends. An argument erupted between them. The fight escalated to the point that the male smashed a large, heavy object over the head of the female, causing her to hit the ground with a serious wound. I immediately jumped into action to give her medical aid. My friend just stood there explaining why her unfaithfulness justified his anger, and after all since she was coming after him with a knife it was self-defense. I told him I didn't care whose fault it was, he needed to call the authorities or I would. He responded that he wasn't calling anybody, that I was a doctor and so I should be able to handle it. At that point I rang 911 and in a short while the EMT workers arrived, along with two police officers. The police officers entered the room, and after looking at the two of us, placed me in handcuffs without so much as asking one question. That was a dream, but from my life experience it could have easily been reality. God doesn't judge Black skin, but our society does, and that is the funkified truth.

THE FUNK OF IT

The British philosopher Michael Oakeshott is said to have believed in the existence of an "aesthetic consciousness," that is, [actualized by] the person who does the seeing."[24] Each of the following chapters will end with a section called "The Funk of It." That section will consist of personalized comments about the preceding subject matter through my eyes, or as Oakeshott made reference, the one doing the seeing. The funk of it is that throughout my entire life the aesthetics of my being has resulted in receiving extra scrutiny in white spaces. That in turn resulted in me having to assuage the fears of people I didn't even know. In Funk circles that would be characterized as "a funky way to treat somebody," and I always wondered why I have had to experience it in the first place.

A couple of mild examples. I have had to stuff my opinions when I would hear my white friends make comments about the grotesque appearance of Black people, especially young Black males. They felt comfortable making jokes about their aesthetic choices such as gold teeth, "weird" hairstyles, loud clothing, etc., as though I agreed with their view. Particularly ironic is that they didn't realize that I was young once and those same sentiments were expressed about my style of dress. Other times a friend would slip and make an off-the-cuff comment about Black people in my presence

24. Podoksik, *Cambridge Companion to Oakeshott*, 95.

39

that would be quickly followed up with "Oh, but you are different." No I was not, nor did I want to be viewed as different! I wanted to be accepted and not have my perceived aesthetic "anomalies," meaning my Blackness, simply overlooked. The other side of the coin is that it is a drag to know that in certain spaces, the very sight of my body is still aesthetically displeasing to so many. I can see it in their eyes.

3

POETICS TO POETHICS

A rt has a moral component built into it and no art form embodies that viewpoint more than poetics. What then is poetics and what are its concerns? The word *poetics* got its start in a treatise written by Aristotle in connection with the dramas popular during his lifetime. For Aristotle, poetics was more than poetry or the script for a play. It included elements of the aesthetics discussed in the previous chapter in addition to music, dance, and the spoken word. When those disciplines are fused, they become what I am calling poetics, giving artistic expression to the concerns of everyday life. Aristotle said that the dramas of his day were presented musically, "until Thespis [an actor] introduced the prologue and the internal speeches. If so, Thespis was the first to interweave choral song with an actor's speeches."[1] Speaking of melding words and music, philosopher Franz Rosenzweig said, "Of all the qualities of a work of art, the most profound is the lyric . . . Of all the arts, music has the reputation of being the most difficult."[2] We can infer from the preceding quotes that at least in the theatrical world, words and music have been inseparable for a very long time.

This chapter is about poetry written for the sake of art, as well as poetry written with a deeper meaning intended by the artist. That is why this chapter is titled "Poetics to Poethics." I am a musician, and, yes, music can be difficult to perform and even difficult to understand, but the message contained in its lyrics (poetry) should not be. The author of *Musicophilia* related a situation where a woman found it challenging to appreciate the melody in music when complex rhythms were added. One might think that

1. Britannica.com, "Thespis," para. 1.
2. Rosenzweig, *Star of Redemption*, 149.

would end with her not caring much for music, but the opposite was true. She said that the reason she was able to get past the confusion that the rhythms caused and appreciate music was because "anything with words is okay."[3] And so it was words that saved the day. This section is partially about the way words are used as lyrics in a strict musical application, but it is also about how words and their meaning influence our perspectives about race.

The prologue to the book *Rebel Music* features a young white woman from Pennsylvania who had relocated to New York City in order to convert to Islam. Upon her arrival she soon became immersed in the city's burgeoning hip-hop scene. The question was asked of this blue-eyed Muslim, "How did a white girl from Pennsylvania become a Muslim named Aziza who organizes turntable battles in the Bronx?"[4] Her answer was simple and direct: "The lyrics brought me here."[5] That is the power of words. For this woman, a complete life change happened as a result of the song lyrics by a hip-hop artist named Grandmaster Flash.

Authors Amos Oz and Fania Oz-Salzberger suggested that it was the use of words that kept the Jewish people together throughout a long and difficult history: "Jewish continuity was always paved with words."[6] Since the dawn of widespread literacy in the West, words have been used to facilitate cohesion and a sense of belonging within a society. African people in the United States were unable to put things down on paper because they were legally forbidden to read and write. They resorted to communicating through songs whose lyrics were both poetry and musical storytelling, that is, poetics. For the enslaved African, a song was more than music, it was a tool to communicate and foster solidarity between a disparate people group in a very unstable environment. Words, in the form of uniquely Black American linguistics, were used to describe the pain and ease the pain. That tradition continues today in the lyrics of rap and hip-hop.

3. Sacks, *Musicophilia*, 112.

4. Hisham, *Rebel Music*, ix.

5. Hisham, *Rebel Music*, ix.

6. Oz and Oz-Salzberger, *Jews and Words*, x.

"POETRY IS . . . FINER THAN HISTORY; FOR POETRY EXPRESSES THE UNIVERSAL"[7]

I agree with the great philosopher Aristotle, who believed that poetry addresses the entire spectrum of the human experience. It would appear that the Elizabethan-era British statesman Sir Philip Sidney believed that too because he said, "Poetry does not simply instruct; it moves the soul toward what it shows."[8] This reinforces my understanding about the importance of poetics as a revealer of what otherwise might be concealed inside the heart. Martin Heidegger said it this way: "the essence of art is poetry . . . the essence of poetry, in turn, is the founding of truth."[9] That brings us to one of the not so pleasant uses of poetry, lament. Lament is the acknowledgment of the funk that life can bring. The funk we are addressing in this chapter is of the *funkiere* variety, meaning the stinky kind. That is why the poetry in the songs of lament we are about to discuss are best interpreted as a form of a "cry, a sigh, a gesture, a reaction by which a living soul seeks to defend itself."[10]

What follows are songs or poems that express that form of lament. The first two are from a song titled "Sal Si Puedes," from a jazz album titled *East Side San Jose* that I recorded with my lifelong friend Clifford Coulter. The others are from the Bible. One of those poems is a Psalm of David penned during a time when God seemed quite distant and unavailable to him. David's poem expresses the same frustration as Clifford's because the anxiety that each writer felt was alienation due to the actions of others. Moreover, the possibility of relief from the underlying causes of their unease seemed remote. Poetics can get to the heart of injustice but should not stop there. As British political theorist Michael Oakeshott stated, "Poetic contemplation . . . requires a willingness to be acted upon."[11] Poetics should affect the heart in ways that release the passion within us to pursue what it is we believe to be important.

7. Brainyquote.com, "Aristotle."
8. Dryness, *Poetic Theology*, 50.
9. Heidegger, *Basic Writings*, 199.
10. Fox, *Poetic Medicine*, 2.
11. Podoksik, *Cambridge Companion to Oakeshott*, 97.

POETICS AS LAMENT

"Sal Si Puedes"

I used to wonder a long time ago,
what it is that makes a rich man rich,
and a poor man be so poor.
How can so few have so much, too much
Then there 're those who have nothing but blues for their mind.
Could it be the color of a man's skin,
that decides what kind of shape he's going to be in?
What is this force that keeps ruining all my plans?
Poverty, ghetto, call it what you want but you get out if you can!

What was the force that troubled Clifford? What is it that troubles so many Black people today? Could it be structural racism, systemic racism, individual racism, institutional racism, overt racism, covert racism? Or, as many put forward, the absence of personal responsibility and effort on the part of those at the bottom? If status according to race is ongoing, when did it start and where did it come from? According to Sylvie Wynter, it started when the scientific world view ascended to primacy, causing "all the colonized darker-skinned natives of the world and the darker-skinned poorer European peoples themselves"[12] to be categorized differently. She added, "The 'new master code,' a purely scientific one, divided the world into the 'selected' and 'dysselected.'"[13] That shift resulted in the elimination of a royalty-based caste system deciding who deserved what, being replaced with a Darwinian inspired idea of racial difference due to upward evolution exemplified in the (less dark-skinned) decision-maker.

"Sal Si Puedes" (continued)

Oh time goes on and on and on you jus' give in,
There is nothing you can do but dress your wounds and try to sleep.
You get some funny kind'a dream that winds up inside you head,
and for a while you're rich and you've got gold for your bed.
Then you open your eyes and look around,

12. McKittrick, *Sylvia Wynter*, 94.
13. McKittrick, *Sylvia Wynter*, 95.

All your dreams have returned politely to the ground.
What is this force that keeps ruining all my plans I don't understand?
Poverty, ghetto, call it what you want but you get out if you can.

Richard Rothstein addresses the underlying realities of Clifford's lament in his excellent book *Color of Law*. In it he quotes sociologist Patrick Sharkey, who said, "Young African-Americans (from thirteen to twenty-eight years old) are ten times as likely to live in poor neighborhoods as young whites—66 percent of African-Americans, compared to 6 percent of whites . . . [Some] 67 percent of African-American families hailing from the poorest quarter of those neighborhoods a generation ago continue to live in such neighborhoods today."[14] By comparison, only 40 percent of whites growing up in a similar environment were still there after reaching adulthood. That is because a higher percentage of young white families have parents who are able to help with a down payment for their first home than Blacks. Time is not the only thing that goes on and on—poverty does too.

Feeling trapped is the epitome of lament because one aspect of it is characterized this way: "Lament is the cry of those who see the truth of the world's deep wounds and the cost of seeking peace."[15] As the *flashpoints* in the Prelude illustrate, the best road to take for African people to keep the peace is the one bearing the street sign that says "do nothing." A lot of time has passed since we recorded *East Side San Jose* and there are many people who would question whether or not those words are even relevant in 2021. If that is you, please consider these sentiments written in the comment section to a YouTube clip of our lament "Sal Si Puedes," posted in 2018.

> It [the East Side] was always the place to avoid when one grew up in Silicon Valley, especially if you were a West Sider. I always did my best to heed those warnings! The place was seriously dangerous compared to the rest of the valley towns, except perhaps East Palo Alto, which was also a battle zone. It's a good thing Blackie did get out while he could, but it's too bad he couldn't have moved to another part of Silicon Valley.[16]

Blackie? Not in 2018, you say? The recent uprisings that have troubled the US have caused me to rethink how much real progress has been made between the time of our recording that song and the YouTube comments.

14. Rothstein, *Color Of Law*, 186.

15. Katongole and Rice, *Reconciling*, 78.

16. Youtube.com, "Clifford Coulter."

It may actually be true that racial tensions did not arrive at our doorsteps just because of the election of any one politician. Maybe they have been bubbling under the surface all along and many people have been unwilling to acknowledge them.

TIME MOVES POETICS TO A POETHICAL QUESTION

If that section of San Jose is not what it once was, judging by the last quote, the racial attitudes of suburbanites have not kept pace with the times. That begs the question, if racism has not been eradicated through all of the conversations, political campaigns, and well-intended initiatives that have come and gone since the founding, then "how long" is a very legitimate question. The lament of "how long" questions both the reasons behind the delay of justice, and also the length of time injustice must be endured by those affected by it.

Lament—Psalm 13

> How long, Lord? Will you forget me forever?
> How long will you hide your face from me?
> How long must I wrestle with my thoughts and day after day have sorrow in my heart?
> How long will my enemy triumph over me?[17]

We recorded *East Side San Jose* in 1970. And the use of the term *ghetto* does have a time stamp on it. However, it is very important to remember that when it comes to racism, history does repeat itself, and it does not seem to have an expiration date. Consider one of the media responses to the civil unrest happening at the time, and the political action taken in response contemporaneous with Clifford's lament. In 1967, a major news periodical offered a headline, "The Negro in America: What Must Be Done."[18] Notice how easy it was for the editorial staff of the magazine to freely objectify an entire people group. In 1968 President Lyndon B. Johnson signed the Safe Streets and Crime Control Act that was purportedly designed to ease

17. Ps 13:1–2, NIV.
18. Smithsonian National Museum, "Newsweek."

tensions in ghettoized neighborhoods. As you read the quote below notice
the similarity between the perception of Black discontent then and now.

> Congress finds that the high incidence of crime in the United
> States threatens the peace, security, and general welfare of the Na-
> tion and its citizens. To prevent crime and to ensure the greater
> safety of the people, law enforcement efforts must be better coor-
> dinated, intensified, and made more effective at all levels of gov-
> ernment. Congress finds further that crime is essentially a local
> problem that must be dealt with by State and local governments if
> it is to be controlled effectively.[19]

Interpreting events through colorized lenses caused many to show
little or no concern about the treatment Blacks were receiving, or even to
acknowledge that any injustice existed. Many people at the time believed
that the social upheavals were simply disgruntled Blacks acting out their
natural criminal inclinations, rather than them voicing legitimate concerns. Even today there are many who react to any dissatisfaction a Black
person articulates with, "What's the problem?" Alice George noted that at
the time many jumped to a conclusion that the unrest was a crime problem
and not a social dysfunction, so, "Instead of considering the full weight of
white prejudice, Americans endorsed rhetoric that called for arming police officers like soldiers and cracking down on crime in inner cities."[20] The
words *effective* and *effectively* were prominently displayed in the legislation
quoted above, which brings these questions to mind. How do you imagine
a police officer's effectiveness is evaluated? Are they graded on making a
low number of arrests, presumably because their effectiveness resulted in
fewer offenders? Or through the recording of a predetermined number of
interactions with the public in order to satisfy performance metrics set by
the department?

19. Hilbink, "Omnibus Crime Control," para. 1.
20. George, "1968," para. 19.

"EVERY TALE CONDEMNS ME AS A VILLAIN"[21]

Lament—Psalm 56

> Be merciful to me, my God,
> for my enemies are in hot pursuit;
> all day long they press their attack.
> My adversaries pursue me all day long;
> in their pride many are attacking me.
> When I am afraid, I put my trust in you.
> In God, whose word I praise—
> in God I trust and am not afraid.
> What can mere mortals do to me?
> All day long they twist my words;
> all their schemes are for my ruin.
> They conspire, they lurk,
> *they watch my steps.*[22]

The subhead above is from a William Shakespeare play and it is also descriptive of the real-life dramas that are being acted out on many of the streets in cities across America. Police on routine traffic stops will ask people that they suspect to be villains a host of non-traffic related questions, only to spin whatever responses are given into a justification to condemn. The following words were written in 2003, which is a significant amount of time before the recent troubles in America surfaced: "Issues arise when, during routine traffic stops, officers ask questions unrelated to the original reason for the stop. Some courts hold that for an officer to justify questioning beyond the original reason for the stop, there must be reasonable suspicion of independent, criminal activity."[23]

Reasonable suspicion is obviously a very low threshold because what is reasonable to one person may not be to the next. A recent case made national headlines when a white officer shot and killed an unarmed person as he fled. Google the name Walter Scott and watch the video and judge for yourself if the shooting was reasonable. These are the basic facts of the encounter as presented in news reports. Walter Scott was pulled over because of a damaged brake light. He then exited the vehicle and ran away from the officer. NBC News reported, "The video shows Slager [the officer] opening

21. Rutherford, "Brief History," 166.
22. Ps 56:1–6, NIV.
23. Lawrence, "Scope of Police Questioning," para. 7.

fire as the unarmed Scott, 50, ran away. Scott was struck multiple times in the back."[24] I am sure that upon learning the facts of this incident that one sector of the community will ask, why did he run? While the other will ask, why was he stopped?

What I believe to be important is the officer shot a person running away from him eight times, and the person doing the running was fifteen to twenty yards away when the officer fired his gun. The officer then claimed his actions were out of fear for his life. His trial ended in a hung jury because one of the jurors said he believed that Slager demonstrated a "brief disturbance in reason"[25] when he shot Scott. Which of these two possibilities do you believe to be the main motivator, heightened fear or heightened anxiety? Just think, the word *reason* was the key in Mr. Slager's favorable judgment of his case. Please understand that it is a different use of the word *reason* in the lament of people in the Black community over these types of cases. Black people want to know the reason why there remains such a deep divide between us. To my white friends who feel that it is a good idea for the police to proactively hold Blacks "in check" in order to feel safer I say, "Black people are not your enemy!" I repeat, "Black people are not your enemy!"

THE N WORD

Sociolinguistics is an academic discipline focused on words and their usage in social contexts. One example of how it works would be examining the word *nigger*. That word has a long, storied, and ignominious past in America. It has crossed social lines and it has meant different things to different groups. Not too long ago there was even a book written titled, *Nigger: The Strange Career of a Troublesome Word*, that chronicled its history in American society. In that book the author quotes a man named Hosea Easton who gives us insight about its most frequent and damaging use by writing, "Nigger is an opprobrious term, employed to impose contempt upon [Blacks] as an inferior race."[26]

Now check out the language that a former slave uses to identify himself when recalling a time when he was stuck in a rainstorm while riding his *master's* horse. "Do you know what happens to dis' nigger if my hoss

24. Chuck, "Michael Slager," para. 6.
25. Kim, "Walter Scott shooting," para. 9.
26. Kennedy, *Nigger*, 5.

stumbles? Right d'eres where I still be [presumably killed]."[27] We see two completely different perceptions regarding the proper use of one word depending on who is using it. I am sure some of you are scratching your head about now, thinking, "I hear Black people use that word all the time in rap records, and I have heard them use it among themselves; and so that proves that it is really not all that bad." However, there is one key word in Mr. Easton's quote that sheds light on why it is such a terrible word and that word is *contempt*. Yes, it was definitely contempt for Black people that was the intent behind the word's usage in the quote. And contempt, when defined as having a feeling of disdain for a person, is certainly behind most of the racial problems that presently exist. The dictionary says that showing disdain means to "consider [someone or something] to be unworthy of consideration,"[28] and to "reject [someone or something] out of pride or superiority."[29] The belief in white superiority juxtaposed with Black unworthiness pretty much sums up the attitudes that have brought us to this point.

CALHOUN-ISMS

No, this section is not about me. It is about a character in an American theatrical comedy (tragedy) called *Amos 'n' Andy*. Ira Berlin wrote that throughout most of our history in America, "The will of the black people [was] to survive . . . not to be dehumanized by dehumanizing circumstances."[30] No clearer example of dehumanization can be found than in a radio show that was popular in the 1940s. *Amos 'n' Andy* consisted of skits that supposedly depicted life in Black America and was broadcast to a mainly white audience. Following the blackface tradition of the traveling circus, and the vaudeville troupes that were popular, the actors who spoke the lines were white people "sounding Black." *Amos 'n' Andy* was extremely popular. Derrick Bell notes, "In the 1950s, the show was converted into a popular television program using . . . black actors"[31]—instead of white actors as had been the case on the radio. But here is where it gets good. "Most [Black actors] were required to attend sessions by white vocal coaches to learn how to

27. Yetman, *Voices from Slavery*, 51.
28. Lexico.com, "Disdain," line 1.
29. Lexico.com, "Disdain," line 2.
30. Berlin, *Making of African America*, 14.
31. Bell, *Gospel Choirs*, 52.

speak like whites imitating blacks."[32] Think through what that last sentence said. I will tell you what comes to my mind. I think that perfectly illustrates what people mean when they use the term *white superiority*.

There was one character in the program that I took a special interest in named Algonquin J. Calhoun. As with the Greek dramas that opened this chapter, the words the actors spoke, and the manner in which they were delivered, had a purpose beyond mere entertainment. In this instance the goal was to present the Black male a specific way. This Calhoun was, "Amos and Andy's shyster lawyer friend . . . [who was a] forever conniving . . . loud talking, buffoon."[33] I have a clear memory about some of the dialogue that I heard on the *Amos 'n' Andy* television show as a youth. I am not sure which characters were involved other than Calhoun, but I am certain of what was said. In the scene a conniving Calhoun not wanting to pay a debt was shown crafting a letter to explain why he was late with a loan payment. He was muttering these words *while* he was writing his letter of apology, "Andy, I woulda' paid ya da money I owed ya, but I done already sealed the envelope." As a kid I remembered it for its humor. Today I remember it for what must have been the intentions of the writers and producers, which was to shape the way Black people understood themselves. The portrayal of Black people through the lens of white media executives continues to this day. Sadly, many of those portrayals are far from accurate.

The reason I have included what should be a forgettable memory in our conversation about poetics is that it demonstrates the way words can be used to shape perception. From the producers' attempt to disguise the true identity of the actors, to promoting stereotype, words were selected with a purpose in mind. Words have done as much or more to cause the racial divide as have laws, violence, and maybe even the ideology of racial superiority. It was through the use of words exchanged in homes, in schools, and between friends, that racist ideologies were codified and then firmly implanted into the nation's psyche. Any effort made to put the brakes on using words in that way has been met with resistance. Some complain that it is policing speech, and they developed a pejorative phrase, "politically correct," to dissuade Black people from pushing back. These people probably do not realize that every day there are scores of racially insensitive and hateful words used as part of common parlance, and they really are in dire need of review.

32. Bell, *Gospel Choirs*, 52.
33. Bell, *Gospel Choirs*, 52.

People that use racially coded language probably think they are just talking and not doing harm to anyone. But the Bible warns us about the improper use of the tongue. The point I want to make here is that some of the opinions about Blacks, and other people of color, were formed through the use of words. That means part of the healing process must come through words too. As we close out the section on poetics, perhaps it would be a good idea to consider looking at "God as poet of the world."[34] Why? Because as Matthew LoPresti has suggested, "A few lines of poetry can distill what might take hundreds of years for theologians to parse."[35] Amos Wilder tells of one other reason that poetics to peoethics is beneficial, commenting, "The Christian imagination, a theopoesis, is necessary in any time to safeguard . . . these dimensions of reality."[36] So let us close with this poem given to us by the master poet.

Ecclesiastes 1:8–10

All things are wearisome,
more than one can say.
The eye never has enough of seeing,
nor the ear its fill of hearing.
What has been will be again,
what has been done will be done again;
there is nothing new under the sun.
Is there anything of which one can say,
"Look! This is something new"?
It was here already, long ago;
it was here before our time.[37]

THE FUNK OF IT

All things are wearisome. That is the lived reality for a great many marginalized people who go unnoticed because nothing about their lives is "newsworthy." And what has been done will be done again unless we make

34. Faber and Fackenthal, *Theopoetic Folds*, 94.
35. Faber and Fackenthal, *Theopoetic Folds*, 94.
36. Wilder, *Theopoetic*, 106.
37. Eccl 1:8–10, NIV.

the hard decisions necessary to prevent it. Remember, the essence of poetry is truth. I want to take you inside my truth. Let us begin by looking at part of the lyrics from a song I wrote a few years ago:

Johnny

Where are you going Johnny, you're out at three a.m.,
Where are you going Johnny, walking at three a.m.?
You used to look like a child, now you got the swagger of a man,
You even walked like a child, now you are swaggerin' like a man.

I grew up in the area of San Jose that the woman characterized as a "war zone" when commenting on the YouTube clip of "Sal Si Puedes." I actually never looked at it as a war zone—it was my home. Even though I was arrested more than once for street fighting, I never considered myself or it to be dangerous. What I saw around me were people trying to make their way in life the best they could. In hindsight the expectations from teachers and other adults for me and my peers were pretty low. One day I asked my wife, who is from a white middle-class background, how many people from her high school did she know that went to prison. The answer was none. Well, I knew scores of them from my school years. To me they were all "good dudes," including one kid who went to juvenile hall in the sixth grade for stabbing a teacher. The reason Don stabbed her was for disrespecting him by putting her hands on him. The way I was raised both of those were a no no—with disrespect being at the top of the list of reasons to go to war with somebody. Now to Johnny.

A few years ago, I along with a friend named Mike Lawrence, developed a music program that we used for summer camps at a facility that housed families in distress. Specifically, women and children that the state had rescued from physically abusive relationships. Because of the severity of the situation the women were in, it was an environment that more resembled a prison complex than a family's home. One of the kids we met our first summer became Johnny in the song. The kid was really cute and gregarious when we first met him. He showed a keen interest in music, and would even stay around after we finished to help load our equipment into the cars. Fast forward about three years. As we drove onto the premises I noticed Johnny was back. However, in the intervening years he had a growth spurt, and with it came a change in attitude. Now he reminded me of myself when I was younger, and the many friends of mine from East San Jose that either went to prison or met death prematurely.

After Mike and I parked our cars I made my way to Johnny in hopes he would join us. When I approached him he didn't even acknowledge my presence. He just stood there doing his best to maintain a tough guy stance. I knew exactly what that was because when I was fifteen I was doing much the same thing. He was bad, and his posture was letting any interested party know it. That is exactly how I was at one time, in fact I used to practice my walk and facial expressions to keep them up to snuff. I wanted respect, and in my surroundings being tough was the way to get it. The thought went through my mind that times have changed, but maybe the game hasn't changed. So I went into *my* long discarded semi-hood persona. That drew a smile from Johnny and he opened up. Once the ice was broken, he showed me a guitar pick we had given him and that he saved for all those years. This emerging "bad dude" came to have his heart melted by a person willing to engage him on his terms. As well as by the gift of a guitar pick. God is both the lover of the world and the poet of the world. Poetry is the language of love. Love does cancel out hate when freely given as I did with Johnny, even though I had to make alterations to my "self" in order to show him love. Proverbs 10:12 says, "Hatred stirs up conflict, but love covers over all wrongs."[38] That is the funk of it, and that is the truth too!

38. Prov 10:12, NIV.

4

DANCE

What comes to mind when you think of the word *dance*? Several possibilities exist, such as a handsome tuxedoed couple gracefully executing synchronized movements of figure eights on an immaculately polished ballroom floor. Or maybe it is a stout man and a petite woman wearing cowboy hats, line dancing. Perhaps it is the choreographed variety that can be seen on a ballet stage or movie screen. Now let us put the word *African* or *Black* before the word *dance*. Does that change the mental picture you had about the way the dancers were moving their bodies? I bet it did. You see, for as long as I can remember, it has been understood that when people were moving their feet and swinging their arms in the air to music, those movements were perceived differently when race was factored in. The dances that Black people enjoyed were thought to be primitive and vulgar, while the dances that people of European descent enjoyed were sophisticated and dignified. That perception seems to have been carried over to one degree or another to this present day.

Pride and Prejudice is one of the most well-respected novels ever written and I have even enjoyed a television adaptation of this nineteenth-century English classic. To give you an idea of the novel's impact, "Two hundred years after it was first published, *Pride and Prejudice* has now sold more than 20 million copies."[1] The story centers around wealth, privilege, and upper-class white people living in Elizabethan England. Two of the characters, the knighted Sir William and a Mr. Darcy, are involved in the following exchange. Sir William: "Do you dance, Mr. Darcy?" . . . "Not if I

---

1. Walsh, "Austen power," line 1.

can help it!"[2] To that Sir William responds, "There is nothing like dancing, after all. I consider it as one of the first refinements of polished societies."[3] And Mr. Darcy replies, "Certainly, sir; and it has the advantage also of being in vogue amongst the less polished societies of the world; every savage can dance."[4]

What that illustrates is that our society has had a racialized perception of something as everyday and universal as dance for quite some time. I bring up the novel and this exchange to highlight the way the tentacles of racialized thinking have made their way into so many different areas of our perceptions. Our society's deep, deep commitment to biological racism is the culprit here and there really is no getting around it. The fact that a harmless pleasure can be construed to be a sign of vulgarity, and I presume inferiority, should not be easily dismissed. One of the more difficult obstacles for people desiring to enter the conversation on race is the belief that Black and white people are so essentially different that similar activities are experienced radically different, even dance.

LET IT LOOSE

"Laissez les bons temps rouler" is a French/Cajun saying that when translated into English means "let the good times roll." The English variant is also the title of a song that I recorded with Dr. John on the *Gumbo* album mentioned in the Introduction to this book. The term could also describe the attitude of thousands of people that descend on the city of New Orleans every year at the same time that Christians begin celebrating Lent. For those of you unfamiliar with Mardi Gras, it is best described as one big street party that began way back in 1582, "when Pope Gregory XIII made it an official holiday."[5] Before going any further I want to point out an irony of ironies. As a minister I understand Lent to be a time of serious reflection on the meaning of Jesus' life, death, and resurrection. People in the Christian community fast, set aside time each day to pray, and also deny themselves various pleasures in order to be in solidarity with Christ's suffering. However, as a Funk musician I have firsthand knowledge that people also use this time period to, well, let loose and let the good times roll. And roll all

2. Goodreads.com, "Jane Austen," line 1.
3. Goodreads.com, "Jane Austen," line 3.
4. Goodreads.com, "Jane Austen," line 4.
5. Johnson, "Laissez les Bon Temps Rouler," line 4.

night long indeed. Let me take you inside a few of my funkiest memories of Mardi Gras.

One year my band, Doctor John and the Nite-Trippers, had a featured spot in the New Orleans Mardi Gras celebrations. What "featured" means is that we were situated on a float and given tons of beads and other items to throw to people as we passed. It was a better time than some to be in the South because Jim Crow was on its last legs, which meant that white and Black people were finally relaxed enough to mix on the streets of the famed French Quarter. Everybody wanted to get close enough to shake my hand and get some beads. People, Black or white, had a huge smile on their face if their eyes made contact with mine. Although once we left New Orleans, it was back to business as usual. I would have to sit in the car while my bandmates went inside restaurants and convenience stores because it was illegal for me to enter. I would be denied hotel accommodations in white areas if I was crazy enough to try. My trying would have forced the other band members to make a choice between staying in the nicer white hotels, or joining me on the black side of town. The point—and it is a very important one to remember—is that when it comes to race, advancement in one area does not always signal victory in others.

That said, this particular Mardi Gras things had loosened up a bit. Of course a special dispensation unknown to me could have been granted to us because of our recent celebrity status. Whatever the reason, "normal" racial restrictions were eased. We sang one song on much of the tour that said, "the big bass drum that led the big parade, all on a Mardi Gras Day"— as the float we were riding slowly made its way through the crowd. That song was in reference to the many brass bands, think mini marching bands at the halftime of a football game, that march in the Mardi Gras parade and whose job it was to get everyone in a dancing mood. That was some kind of party and Dr. John and the Nite-Trippers would take that Mardi Gras celebration on the road to places as diverse as Vienna, Austria, a.k.a. "The City of Music," nicknamed in honor of its roots in sophisticated classical music—and to an annual rodeo named the Calgary Stampede in Alberta, Canada. I know there are many that see a Black person functioning in a high-profile position and point to that as proof of improving race relations. Do not be quick to be one of them. History has shown that a few Blacks having really good jobs does not always translate to the uplift of the majority. But back to Mardi Gras.

During our performances Dr. John, and most often singers Robbie Montgomery and Jessie Smith, would second line dance their way on to the stage mimicking the Mardi Gras dancers made up of "a ragtag group behind the band that waves handkerchiefs to the beat of the drum, while a grand marshal in a snazzy suit and jaunty hat leads the way—out-dancing, out buck-jumping them all as he waves his feathered fan."[6] Entertainment journalist Ian McNulty noted that, "Second lines trace their roots back to the 19th century and the fraternal societies and neighborhood organizations that collectively provided insurance and burial services to members, especially among the African-American community."[7] Whatever its roots were, the second line was a time of joyous celebration and dance was a major part of it. In fact some argue that dance as an art form even helped usher in an entire genre of music. "Unlike most of today's jazz, early jazz was intended for dancing, not listening. From Congo Square to elaborate ballrooms, dancing was our way of life!"[8]

RHYTHMIC JOY

Dance is comprised of rhythm patterns expressed bodily, and they can be positive, negative, or both. Dance can be improvisational, where one person expresses themselves, and it can be interactive with a partner. In the latter mode, one feels and senses "the other" and then each dancer adjusts their movements to achieve unity. There is also a dance that is done in a group that is not necessarily improvisational. That dance form is highly choreographed, and the intended goal is to not only create unity with one partner, but unity with a group of partners. Being restricted to the dance steps of a group may not be viewed as that appealing to our individualistic culture. That is because Western culture's individualistic bent even carries over to the way we dance. Consider the way this man from India characterized the way we dance: "Notice how in American clubs people dance whichever way they want with no regard to how others are dancing? This is a distinct characteristic of an individualistic culture."[9]

Wherever I performed during the dance hall and nightclub era of my Funk career, the dances I observed people doing were independent of a

6. Neworleans.com, "The Second Line," line 1.

7. McNulty, "Block Parties," para. 6.

8. Welsh, "Funky Butt," para. 13.

9. Kakade, "Decode A Culture," para. 13.

partner, meaning the actual movements of the dancers did not need to be in synch with the other, even when done in pairs. Dances like the Twist, Boogaloo, the Pony, and the Swim all became popular during America's post-war march down the road to the isolated and independent self being viewed as the best path to happiness. However, that understanding is not so readily accepted in non-Western societies such as India, Africa, Asia, and throughout the southern portion of the Western world in places like Belize, Central America. In those cultures the "we" frequently supersedes the "me." Let us visit one of those localities.

DANCE TO THE RHYTHM OF THE PUNTA

Punta Rock is the name of a music genre in Belize. The original form of Punta music was a style developed by the Garifuna, who lived in the southern part of the country. Over time that style was fused with the rock rhythms from America and the reggae rhythms from Jamaica to produce Punta Rock. A *Huffington Post* travel expert wrote, "If you're lucky enough to be in Belize on Nov. 19, don't be surprised to see thousands of Garifuna parading, partying, dancing and otherwise celebrating their Afro-Caribbean/French/British roots. That day is their annual 'Garifuna Settlement Day,' marking the settlement of the villages long ago on the beaches of Belize."[10] I have been fortunate enough to have witnessed eight and one-half years of Belizean festivities and I came to view them as a display of national pride combined with a unified celebration of life itself.

But wouldn't you know it, one woman in our church had to racialize that joyous celebration by placing some of the dance movements in the vulgar column. She expressed her disapproval of the way darker-skinned Belizeans, and specifically Garifuna people, danced by saying this to my wife, "Oh g'yal they look so funny shaking their big rear ends." Julaine and I looked at each other in utter amazement. That was because our congregant had a well-endowed posterior that was at least equal in size to the average darker-skinned Belizean's. In this instance, and perceptions aside, our dear friend should not have been the person commenting on somebody else's healthy posterior, whether it was dancing or not.

---

10. Schulman, "Shake Your Booty," line 9.

DANCE AS THERAPY

Traditionally dance has offered a type of release for oppressed people. Dance critic Zita Allen offered some interesting insights about the way African slaves put it to use. "They danced for themselves and one another. It was the end of a day spent picking somebody else's cotton, cleaning somebody else's house, caring for other folks' children. This was their time to come together and thank God they had survived another day."[11] Allen added, "Every part of their bodies danced, from their shuffling feet and bent knees to their churning hips and undulating spines, swinging arms, and shimmying shoulders . . . to reveal faces filled with the joy and the ecstasy of dance."[12] Several times I have experienced that feeling playing Funk. On more than one occasion I have been so overcome by emotion playing my bass, that it could only be described as me losing myself in the music. Actually, I felt as though my instrument was playing itself, which is why I identify so easily with Allen's characterization of the emotions Africans experienced as they danced.

Nicole Monteiro and Diana Wall suggested some additional reasons why dance was so important to slaves. "Dance creates an intersubjective space where individuals, whether acquaintances or strangers, enter into intimate relations with each other . . . [and] through this space, individual differences are often times melded into one collective feeling and experience."[13] Contrary to my congregant's opinions, dance was providing that sense of Black unity for the Garifuna people on the streets of Belize and it was wonderful to behold. Witnessing Black joy at P-Funk concerts also helped me to better understand the depth and beauty that is African American dance. Even better, perhaps the dancing I witnessed was similar in style and function to the Ring Shout dance from the slavery era that Zita Allen was referring to earlier. As we are about to learn, Black dance is not primitive, vulgar, or base—it is a highly developed form of artistic expression, worthy of respect.

11. Allen, "Free To Dance," para. 6.

12. Allen, "Free To Dance," para. 2.

13. Monteiro and Wall, "African Dance," 239.

BUCK DANCIN'

Dancing for Black people of my generation was more than a social activity. Dances were a time to showcase our artistic inclinations. For the guys, dance also facilitated a means to compete for female attention. In high school a guy named Biggie would meticulously choreograph all of his dance moves with his partner in order to send a signal that he was just a little cooler than the rest of us. Sure, many of my other friends would practice their moves individually too, but more in keeping with the way a boxer or golfer trains, meaning attempting to perfect traditional movements rather than attempting to create new ones. One scientist noted that a similar use of dance occurs in the animal world, writing, "Impressive is the male blue manakin, which can be found in the forests of Argentina. It spends 90 percent of its waking day, for most of the year, in a dancing duel. Its dancing skills matter: females mate only with the best and most expert male dancers."[14] I have seen that up close and personal because I didn't dance in school, and you can imagine the result of that.

When a brother, meaning insider, would become very proficient, we would say so and so was at the party and man he was "buck dancin'" up a storm. We understood that the use of the term "buck" was a compliment. It was an allusion to what happens in the animal kingdom when the virile males of a species were deemed to be "good bucks." In my neighborhood we used the term *buck* to signal machismo, which in our world automatically brought respect. For example, strong athletes, good fighters, or the guy that all of the women thought was handsome, would often wind up with the nickname "Buck." One example of this would be the famous Los Angeles Laker basketball player Earvin "Magic" Johnson, whose teammates called him Buck "ever since he was a rookie."[15]

BUTT ARE YOU REALLY SURE IT'S REALLY BUCK?

I want to tell you a story about how buck dancing became butt dancing, and how with that came an overtone of perceived racial superiority. Several years ago I worked with a white colleague at a church and we often talked music, particularly my past involvement touring with bands. One day I alluded to the fact that I enjoyed playing with Leon's Creation more than

14. Goymer, "Bird Behavior," para. 6.
15. Ostler, "Here's A Team," para. 8.

some of the other bands. I added that it was because we weren't into "buck dancing" to promote our music like many of the Funk bands of the era. He turned his head and corrected me by saying, "You mean butt dancing, don't you?" I responded with a polite, "No, no, I mean buck dancing." I then made eye contact with him only to see a look I knew only too well. That look was the look of a person doubting either my truthfulness or my knowledge.

My friend asked presumptively, "Are you sure?" One by-product of the ideology of white superiority is the assumption that white knowledge and experience is superior to that of Blacks. That presumption is not usually stated outright, and it may be no more intentional than being one of those things that is simply taken for granted, like two plus two equals four. If a disagreement about a fact should enter a conversation, I have a responsibility to acknowledge the probability that they have a better handle on the truth, and I should concede. I am sure some of you are thinking, "Maybe he is just overly sensitive." To that I can assure you it has happened far too many times to be a misread or coincidence. If the two sentences in quotation marks resonated with you in some way I would simply ask that you consider the possibility that yesterday's master/slave relationship might still influence the way some believe Black and white people *should* relate to each other.

Bruce Baker said, "Buck dancing is a folk dance that originated among African-Americans during the era of slavery . . . The original buck dance, or 'buck and wing,' referred to a specific step performed by solo dancers."[16] Now, consider this. The first reference that popped up on my screen when I Googled "butt dancing" was a YouTube clip that depicted a woman bouncing on a ball in a spoof on a workout video. That video was from Brazil and it was immediately followed by another clip from Korea. The entire first page of my Google search contained no references outside of those two, just repeats. Now you can see why I am confident that my friend mistakenly believed buck dancing was somehow connected to the phrase "butt naked." To prevent you from ever making my friend's mistake, "In contemporary usage, 'buck dancing' often refers to a variety of solo step dancing to fiddle-based music done by dancers primarily in the Southern Appalachians."[17] Lighthearted dance analogies aside, unintentional race-based assumptions

16. Baker, "Buck Dancing," para. 1.
17. Baker, "Buck Dancing," para. 2.

seem to always lead to a great deal of misunderstanding, often with not so happy endings.

DANCING IN THE STREETS

I played bass for Martha Reeves, who recorded the megahit "Dancing in the Street." The recent racial unrest in the US has brought a new context for the lyrics, "Summer is here and the time is right for dancing in the street." Yes, the summer heat should bring to mind a different type of heat because many of our cities burned in protest to a perceived unbroken chain of racial oppression. Consider one of the earlier links of that chain that occurred during African colonialism. We find stories about tribes that developed dance as a way to deceptively protest against the invaders from Europe. One of the methods used was, "a strategy [employed] . . . was the use of the cultural symbols of dance, song, and art, which were often unintelligible to colonial officials."[18] Indeed, "In many East African colonies, dance associations were organized, and the associations created dance forms in which colonial officials were ridiculed [without their realizing it]."[19] I am sure the people unfamiliar with their customs assumed their dancing to be consistent with the mental picture of African people they had invented for themselves. And that being the one where Africans were portrayed as childlike and submissive, not knowing the reverse was happening right before their eyes. The dance was meant to protest as well as subvert the colonial imposition on their lives.

Dancing as protest did not only happen in "primitive" Africa during times gone by. Dancing as protest is happening right here and right now. One British newspaper recorded this example. "The protests sparked by the killing of George Floyd have spread across the world and as many have said: this is not a moment, it's a movement. But it is also a moment of movement, as the protests have been accompanied by outbreaks of dancing . . . [because] dance and protests have long gone hand in hand."[20] A journalist writing about the protests following George Floyd's recent death noted, "after the dancing came a silent, nine-minute knee—[and this] is just one instance of dance intersecting with protest over the past two weeks of global

18. Boahen, *African Perspectives,* 80.
19. Boahen, *African Perspectives,* 80.
20. Roy, "How The Electric Slide," para. 1.

demonstrations against racism and police brutality."[21] This dancing in the streets was not a time of partying as with Martha Reeves, but a unified effort to "re-embody" Blackness with the "Black soul" in a way that matters.

DANCE AS JURISPRUDENCE

Zora Neale Hurston interviewed one of the last surviving enslaved people born in Africa in the early 1900s. Her book *Barracoon* is a compilation of interviews she had done with a man named Cudijo Lewis—whose given name prior to being brought to the US was Kossola. One of the stories that he recounted describes the process his tribe used when they executed someone convicted of murder. The execution involves a machete and an elaborately choreographed set of dance steps performed by the executioner. Chiefs from the neighboring villages are there to sit in and are involved in making the final judgment about the fate of the accused. The trial ends with the king of the entire tribe being the final arbiter. What follows is how Lewis describes the part of the process that is relevant to our discussion:

> De executioner dance until he get de sign of de hand [from one of the chiefs]. Den he dance up to the murderer and touch his breast with the point of de machete. He dance away an' de next time he touch the man's neck with the knife. The third time dat he touch de man, other men rush out and seize the murderer an' take-a de palm cord and stretch him face to face upon the dead man [victim] an' tie him tight so he cain move hisself.[22]

Before anyone jumps to the conclusion that all this does is provide more evidence that the African was in need of being civilized by the European, recall that Europeans had people drawn and quartered with the executed person's entrails dragged about the city. They burned people alive and beheaded others in the public square and placed the severed heads on display for all to see, including children. The list goes on. In 2020 while the US is still executing people, the only conversation happening about the process is centered around finding the most humane way to put someone to death. My main point here is that the method used to put someone to death may be more grotesque than humane, no matter how it is carried out. One interesting sidenote to me is that the coronavirus pandemic has resulted

21. Burke, "Dancing Bodies," para. 3.
22. Walker and Hurston, *Barracoon*, 31.

in a momentary pause in executions in most states. One can only wonder why. At a minimum, that inconsistency could lead one to think that if a virus can put a halt to executing people, maybe it is not all that necessary in the first place.

DANCE—COMMUNICATION AND RITUAL HEALING

Nicky Clayton, a biologist and psychologist, observed that "communicating via motion is common to both dance and the natural world."[23] An example of that is that when I was a kid, it was understood that many European people used their hands for emphasis when speaking. In that case the fact that a body part was used to communicate was never viewed as evidence of racial inferiority. The authors of a book on West African spirituality noted, "We tell stories through our music and dance that reveal our histories and purpose for our lives . . . We heal through our music and dance."[24] It is also worth noting that healing through ritual that often includes dance is a major part of the African understanding of good health care. The authors of *Experiencing Ritual* note that "to be effective . . . all of the following elements were indispensable: the patient, the doctor, medicines . . . singing, drumming, and dancing."[25] One thing is for sure, dancing has value way beyond its entertainment value. That makes it easy to see why Africans love dance, and people of African descent do too.

LIFE LESSONS FROM DANCE

For as long as I can remember dance has been more than just entertainment for Black people. That is because life in a society that racializes so much of its cultural understanding about who we are, resulted in dance becoming one more tool to use in the fight to have our identity defined the way we would like it. There have been many who have agreed with Sir William that black dance is "savage." There have been times when those same people enjoyed watching us dance merely to prove their perceived superiority. Check out what a Yankee soldier told a freed slave named Sarah Debro. She recounts that she was sitting on the porch of her former slave

23 Goymer, "Bird Behaviour," para. 1.
24. Doumbia and Doumbia, *Way of The Elders*, 96.
25. Turner, *Experiencing Ritual*, 17.

master's home when the Yankee soldiers arrived on the scene. After a brief period of questioning about the whereabouts of some gold by the soldier "he pushed me off the step and said if I don't star dancing he gwine shoot my toes off. As scared as I was, I sure did some shufflin.'"[26]

THE FUNK OF IT

There was a time when the Father of Funk James Brown resorted to dance as a means to ingratiate himself with white people. Nelson George wrote, "His childhood and early career were defined by the restrictions of segregation . . . Brown was just another dirt-poor Negro boy dancing for money in a redneck town."[27] George went on to say that James Brown "somehow cultivated strong self-esteem within a system devised to quell just such a quality." Yes, the fact is things are better today than the slavery days. And things are better than even the Jim Crow days of James Brown's youth. However, we are not completely past the stereotypes attached to dance. In fact, I would say we are still quite a distance away. But "a recent discovery shows that our [individual] dance style is almost always the same, regardless of the type of music, and a computer can identify the dancer with astounding accuracy."[28] You have to wonder if a computer will soon be able to identify the dancer's race, or does that require the subjectivity of the human brain just as racism does?

Meet Barry "Frosty" Smith and Buddy Miles. If you are not familiar with the names, they were both drummers that played with me when I recorded with the Funkadelic. Buddy's most notable musical project was being part of Jimi Hendrix's Band of Gypsies, while Frosty has played with everyone from Sly Stone to Stevie Ray Vaughn. What is of interest here is that they were both powerhouse drummers and they were both extremely overweight at some point in their lives. However, in spite of all the extra weight they carried, they were as light on their feet as a feather and excellent dancers. Now comes the fly in the racially stereotyped bowl of soup. Frosty was white and Buddy was Black. That's right, two famous drummers who were "racially different" shared an innate ability to dance. That is how the ideology of race works, doesn't it? A racialized view of humanity finds difference where none exists. And that really is the funk of it.

26. Yetman, *Voices from Slavery*, 99.

27. George and Leeds, eds., *James Brown Reader*, 1.

28. University of Jyväskylä, "The way you dance," para. 1.

Part Two

THE SCIENTIFIC MIND

"Ethics and science need to shake hands."

—RICHARD CABOT

5

COGNITION AND RACE

Cognition is the process we engage in that leads to the knowledge we rely on. This chapter presupposes that this process needs reevaluating from time to time. As you read this chapter be aware that many people use the word *cognition* interchangeably with *consciousness*. But this section is not so much about the type of consciousness philosophers debate, or the operations of the brain that the neuroscientists probe as the aftereffects of our knowledge. This means we will not be spending much time examining how we come to know certain things, but reconsidering what it is we think we know. In matters of race, a willingness to take a personal inventory from time to time is crucial. Most people do not see the need to do that. They know what they know and are satisfied with leaving it there.

Bridging Austin is the name of our church and it exists as a reconciling community. At one of our Bridging meetings I shared a recent experience when a white person was extremely rude to me. A friend, who is a white professional, challenged me by saying that my treatment might not have been due to race. I vigorously pushed back because I was 100 percent certain it was. But she *knew* she was right. One of our cardinal rules at Bridging is that we do not judge the intentions or experiences of the other. Recently a Black woman based in London named Otegha Uwaghba wrote a book titled *Whites,* in which she shared her impressions of life as a person of African descent living in white British culture. Many of her white critics were offended by her characterizations. They reacted that way without ever considering that, wrong or right, what she had written were *her* perceptions resulting from *her* experiences—and that criticizing them was tantamount to invalidating them. What should be remembered as we move forward is that there are certain experiences that simply will not be common to all. In matters of race, they cannot be.

The authors of a book titled *Critical Race Theory* chimed in on the difficulties involved in making hard judgments in similar circumstances, noting, "They [similar experiences to mine] can be thought of as small acts of racism, consciously or unconsciously perpetrated, welling up from the assumptions about racial matters most of us absorb from the cultural heritage in which we come of age in the United States."[1] Neuroscientist Michael Graziano offered an observation that might help us avoid this practice when he wrote, "My central scientific point is that you never do experience another person's mind . . . You experience a model that your brain constructs."[2] What is important to remember is that the racialized constructs formulated inside of our brains will produce consequences for others. That is why we need to be willing to examine what it is we think.

THINK

Cognitive science focuses on the mind and the way we process information. A paper written by Sujita Kumar Kar and Meha Jain used a large circle resembling a wheel to illustrate the major domains of cognition that comprise cognitive science. From that list I will be touching on "attention, memory, judgment, and social cognition."[3] I mention this because knowledge, or at least what we consider knowledge, consists of several mental processes. In my first book I coined the umbrella term *racial cognition* to describe the way cognitive science and race intersect. "[Racial cognition] happens when a person becomes overly cognizant or aware of race, and they run every thought about, or impression of, another human being through a racially coated filter."[4] Richard Swinburne noted how this type of knowledge is often the result of "the beliefs we acquire through experience, memory, and testimony."[5] Those are a few of the ingredients used to lay the groundwork for errant hypotheses such as racial cognition. All of this is to say that what people think about race runs very deep and very wide. However, that does not mean that what people think about race cannot be deeply wrong.

1. Delgado et al., *Critical Race Theory*, 2.
2. Graziano, *God, Soul, Mind, Brain*, 49.
3. Kar and Jain, "Current understandings," fig. 1.
4. Calhoun, *Rhythm and Grace*, 52.
5. Swinburne, *Mind, Brain, and Free Will*, 58.

With that in mind, let us attempt to get our collective racial cognition wheels rolling. What follows is a sampling of the descriptors that white people have used for me during my lifetime: negro, colored, Black, and person of color. Today people believe they are being accurate when they call me an African American. Take a hard look at this picture of the African continent.

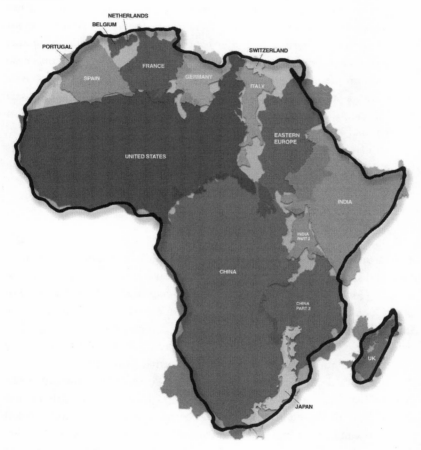

The picture indicates that the following countries would fit on the land mass that comprises Africa: the US, India, China, France, Portugal, Germany, Eastern Europe, Spain, Japan, and the UK. Now consider this: "Africa covers about one-fifth of the world's land area . . . and is divided into 53 independent countries and protectorates . . . There are over 800 ethnic groups in Africa, each with its own language, religion, and way of life."[6] Now think about the picture that comes to your mind of what an African American should look like. Are you sure that is accurate? Look at the above figure a little closer. From which one of the 800 ethnic groups would your picture of an African American have originated? See the problem?

The famous British detective Sherlock Holmes once told his side-kick Doctor Watson, "It is a capital mistake to theorize before one has data. Insensibly one begins to twist facts to suit theories, instead of theories to fit facts."[7] There is no better example of twisting facts to support a theory than when the subject is race. To get human beings to become totally committed to the idea of separate and distinct races requires media saturation, a supportively interpreted historical record, and some loosely formed scientific theory to validate it. Steven Shapin suggested in a section of his book *Never Pure* that some of what we think we know may just be "an artifact of communication."[8] What that says to me, as it relates to race, is that much of the knowledge people use to categorize others is often nothing more than racialized gossip.

THINK AGAIN

Several years ago a New York newspaper ran a headline saying that a Bushman had shared a cage with some apes. What it was referring to was a time when a Congolese man named Otis Benga had been put on display with other "creatures from the jungle," such as apes and snakes, inside a cage in a zoo. This human being was devalued to the point of becoming a zoo exhibit. That was done to satisfy the curiosity of white New Yorkers who were curious about what "lower" animal forms from Africa looked like. This was considered acceptable because many Americans believed that Mr. Bengo "happened to be a Bushman, one of a race that scientists do not rate high on the human scale."[9] The basic understanding that undergirded that view can be seen in this opinion given by an archaeologist at the time, "The black, the brown, and the red races differ anatomically . . . from the white."[10] When we rely on pseudoscience that "treats the social world as

6. Newworldencyclopedia.org, "African dance," para. 3.

7. Sherlockholmesquotes.com, line 6.

8. Shapin, *Never Pure*, 91.

9. Newkirk, *Spectacle*, 13.

10. Newkirk, "Man who was caged," para.14.

a reflection of the natural world . . . there are consequences . . . such as natural hierarchies existing between races."[11] Rest assured those ideas have not completely died out.

Mr. Bengo was caged at a time when Darwinian evolutionary theory had just become the darling of the scientific community. It was a time when statements such as "That the Negro is more like a monkey than the European . . . cannot be denied as a general observation"[12] would be accepted as pure fact. Although most people today would never say such a thing in public, I am very confident many believe that science *has* proven their race is higher on "the scale of evolution" than others. However, geneticist Adam Rutherford discovered a very interesting bit of information about Charles Darwin. He stated that at the time Darwin sketched his evolutionary tree in his notebook, he had little access to any human remains to base his ape-to-man theory on. "How these ancient apes fitted onto the human tree was entirely unknown . . . 'I think' he scrawled at the top of that notebook."[13] Take a moment to consider the amount of pain and suffering African people have endured due in large part to a theory grounded in two words, "I think . . ."

STRAIGHT TALK

Let us look a little closer at Africa and examine some other common misperceptions. What most of us know today, or think we know, about Africa are facts such as the fight to end apartheid by notables like Nelson Mandala and Desmond Tutu. Or we know that it is a large "country" where starvation, violence, corruption, and disease run rampant. If those perceptions are even close to being accurate they are certainly recent occurrences. Were you aware that until 1880 the continent of Africa was not under the colonial rule of European powers? Then without African knowledge or consent a conference was held in Berlin where several European countries carved up "ownership" of the land, and in doing so, assumed total control of its people. A short while later the "race" was on between European powers to see who would get the upper hand in securing the most prime real estate and other resources. That race ended with most of the African continent being under European control.

11. Daynes and Lee, *Desire for Race,* 3.

12. Gossett, *Race,* 57.

13. Rutherford, *Brief History,* 18.

A teacher of African history and culture at King's College London named Toby Green observed, "Stereotypically, Westerners have seen Africa as 'the continent without history.'"[14] However, an African named Philani A. Nyoni said this about that non-history: "Africa had its own forms of commerce, science, art and other measures of civilization long before the arrival of the colonizers."[15] Colonization was not the result of an invitation, it was a conquest, and it was an extremely violent conquest at that. A. Adu Boahen writes, "All imperial powers developed professional armies and police which they used to occupy and police their colonies."[16] One of the tribes named the Maji resisted and that resulted in "75,000 dead, while the uprising in south-west Africa led to a loss of life of about half its [British Nigeria] colony."[17] I don't know about you, but that kind of disregard for human life catalyzes the elements that my tears are made of.

Another example of the utter disregard for African humanity can be seen in the escapades of a man named King Leopold of Belgium. He was responsible for the killing of millions of Black Congolese, while subjugating the people and extracting all of the material wealth that was located beneath African soil. He has had the dubious honor to be a called a mass murderer equal to Adolf Hitler. In Europe there was a debate as to the actual number of deaths that he was responsible for, but a Belgium anthropologist named Daniel Vangroenweghe noted, "Talk of whether Leopold killed ten million people or five million is beside the point, it was still too many."[18] The book King Leopold's Ghost, which chronicles all of the horrors that went on in the Congo, ends with a chapter titled "The Great Forgetting." His atrocious behavior has been forgotten largely because Westerners turned a blind eye to the brutality in real time. The fact remains, his outlandish policies were swept under a metaphorical rug made up of the bodies of millions of Black Africans. To add insult to injury, a statue was erected in Antwerp to honor him. Shame on him, and shame on us!

I speculate that one of the reasons that King Leopold's contribution to the hall of shame slipped beneath the radar screen of the average European was because of the ethnicity of those that suffered. Let us look at a few examples of what people in the Congo endured during Leopold's reign of

14. Green, "Africa in its fullness," para 17.
15. Thisisafrica.me, "What Africa Had," para. 1.
16. Boahen, *African Perspectives*, 99.
17. Boahen, *African Perspectives*, 99.
18. Bates, "Hidden Holocaust," para. 18.

terror. In addition to being brutally murdered, Africans had their limbs cut off when they did not perform their forced labor "assignments" in a manner that Europeans saw fit. Africans lived through the humiliation of being forced to work twelve-hour shifts under conditions of starvation on the land of their ancestors' birth. All to enrich a person they would never see or meet, King Leopold. Of course, he did not see himself as a murderer or even a terrorist. He saw himself as a civilizer of savages. Despotic behavior always begins with the dehumanization of the other, and is typically masked with an "all in the name of progress" narrative.

For example, King Leopold "presented himself as a philanthropist eager to bring the benefits of Christianity, Western civilization, and commerce to African natives."[19] I am sure many European Christians mistakenly believed he was doing exactly that. And that illustrates the power of a well-crafted story. A "civilizer of savages" was the story presented to me in school about Henry Morgan Stanley, who was King Leopold's emissary. He was depicted as a heroic figure who overcame unimaginable obstacles to uplift a primitive people. That was what I thought I knew about him for decades. Later I learned he killed hundreds of Africans on his way to finding a doctor named Livingstone. His famous line, "Doctor Livingstone I presume," cemented his hero status in the minds of millions in Europe and America. But the picture painted of him as an explorer and humanitarian is far from accurate. Stanley recorded the following example of his "exploratory style" in his journal: "We have attacked and destroyed 28 large towns and three of four score villages."[20]

Other entries in his private journal contained words that reveal the way he really perceived the African people and his relationship to them: "the blacks give an immense amount of trouble, they are too ungrateful to suit my fancy."[21] Ungrateful? Let that sink in for a moment. In a letter to King Leopold, Stanley stated that chains were a better punishment for insubordination on the part of the Africans because it could be done "without disfiguring or torturing the body."[22] I wonder what one had to do to be insubordinate? Are there parallels creating headlines in the news today? History, like race science, can be a home to many things that are simply not true. There have always been alternative stories available but it requires

19. Hochschild, "Leopold II," para. 3.
20. Hochschild, *King Leopold's Ghost,* 49.
21. Hochschild, *King Leopold's Ghost,* 31.
22. Hochschild, *King Leopold's Ghost,* 67.

work to seek them out. Plato believed that it is possible to "move from unconscious deception to see what it is that deceives us."[23] Unfortunately human pride being what it is, admitting that we may have acted on some faulty narratives from both science and history seems to be a very difficult thing to do.

TELL THE TRUTH—EVEN IF YOU'VE GOTTA MAKE IT UP!

Let us leave Africa and turn the spotlight towards Australia. The subhead above is my take on an old Australian saying that says telling a good story is more important than the truth. One story that circulated the globe concerning the treatment of the indigenous people of Australia was that laws were passed to "care" for the natives. This snippet from a *Britannica* article illustrates the mind-set of the colonizers: "They [the "natives"] were put into reserves and given food and clothing to 'smooth the dying pillow' as they awaited what the Europeans took to be cultural extinction."[24] Why such cruelty? A 1916 issue of *National Geographic* placed the following words beneath the photos of two Aboriginal people: "South Australian Blackfellows: These savages rank lowest in intelligence of all human beings."[25] At the time the science of phrenology, which was "the detailed study of the shape and size of the cranium as a supposed indication of character and mental abilities,"[26] was huge in Australia. The Australian "settlers" used the research harvested from this scientific discipline to prove that the native Aboriginals they were displacing were so inferior that they were incapable of controlling their own destinies.

There was also a connection between America's race theory and the Australian variety. The connection can be seen in that they decided to call aboriginal men Jim Crows. Remember, "Jim Crow" was "a derisive slang term for a black man and America's segregationist policies bore that name . . . It came to mean any state law passed in the South that established different rules for blacks and whites . . . Jim Crow laws were based on the theory of white supremacy."[27] In 1862, an Australian man named Hamilton "had

23. Louth, *Origins of Christian Mystical*, 5.
24. Britannica.com, "Aboriginal Peoples," para. 4.
25. Mao, "National Geographic," para. 3.
26. Lexico.com, "Phrenology."
27. Crf-usa.org, "Brief History of Jim Crow," para. 5.

[aboriginal] Jim Crow's skull and was using it in his lectures to demonstrate features he considered criminal."[28] Note that criminality was believed to be an observable physical characteristic. Have we really moved past that kind of thinking?

It should not come as a surprise to learn that race theories in the West are a shared commodity. People who are looking for proof to justify their position will often glom onto any bizarre theory they can find. Phrenology never gained much traction in the US, but it did manage to get a foothold into the thinking of educators in a few northern states. Some of them decided that it made sense not to educate Black children due to their limited cranial capacities and the "science" to confirm the wisdom in their policies was soon forthcoming. A French scientist named Louis Pierre Gratiolet "advanced a theory that in Negroes the coronal structure of the skull closes at an early age, gripping the brain in a prison and arresting its growth."[29] That belief could be why many states passed laws against teaching slaves to read. But the folly in racialized thinking was exposed when they turned right around and used the fact that Blacks were uneducated as proof of their racial inferiority. Circular logic such as that is still happening when it comes to race. For example, there are many people that accept theories such as the "bell curve" as legitimate science without questioning the premises on which they are based. *The Bell Curve*'s authors used the scores of intelligence tests as proof of biological racial difference.[30] They reached their conclusions without ever considering who developed the tests, or who decided what types of questions would be used to determine intelligence.

A DEEPER PROBLEM

I had a physical a few years ago and to my surprise the files at my doctor's office had me listed as white. How the error came to light was that I underwent a blood test that included a kidney function test. A short while later I received an email telling me to come in for a follow-up because my tests revealed that I was in stage 3 kidney failure. My doctor went through some diet advice and asked if I wanted to be referred to a nephrologist. Julaine and I were pretty concerned, and so I scoured the Internet with the hope of finding the best course of action. I have kept all of my physical printouts

28. Smith, "Skull," para. 18.
29. Gossett, *Race,* 75.
30. Herrnstein and Murray, *Bell Curve.*

since the 1990s and so I decided to compare the results of the past three years to gauge how rapidly the disease was advancing. I went to the file, looked at my 2017 results, and then noticed in the left-hand corner of the paper that I was listed as white. It was funny, but the fact that I am not white had meaning, and a scientific meaning at that.

The National Kidney Foundation had this to say about the methodology my doctor based her diagnosis on: "Glomerular filtration rate (GFR) is the best overall index of kidney function. Normal GFR varies according to age, sex, and body size, and declines with age."[31] There is one word that is missing in the last sentence and that is *race*. Race science does come into play with kidney disease diagnostically. In spite of the well-established fact that, "Of the total biological variation found in samples taken around the world 90 to 95 percent . . . occurs within 'racial' categories and only 5 to 10 percent between them,"[32] the GFR had two different metrics, one for white and another for Black. In this instance my "Black" numbers suggested that I was in stage 2 kidney disease, meaning in the safe range. Whereas my "white" numbers, even though they are actually the same, put me in the more serious stage 3 category. I hope it strikes you as kind of creepy that even where someone's health is involved, medical science can find racial division.

We should not gloss over the fact that there is more variation within the white group, meaning between themselves, than there is between white and Black groups in general. That means that a white person is more apt to be more genetically different from another white person than she or he is from a Black person. So how did kidney experts arrive at creating different scales based on what amounts to be at the most a 10 percent difference? They looked at the disproportionate number of Blacks suffering from the disease as compared to whites. And rather than attributing the difference to either diet, economic stressors, exercise habits, or other behaviors, they decided the reason must be due to skin color. My experience is a perfect example of scientists observing the natural world, and then developing a scientific finding to correspond to their assumptions. My point is this: not all science is objective or racially neutral. Science, like every other area of our society, has been affected by the ideology of race. That is because, as

31. Kidney.org, "GFRF Calculator."
32. Wade, *Race*, 90.

Angela Saini has written, "scientists are socialized human beings who live within a society and their ideas are [often] social constructions."[33]

EMPTYING DES-CARTES

As we close it is important that we revisit some of what was said at the beginning of this chapter. That is because in conversations related to race the number one impediment to progress is a variation of one simple sentence, "I don't believe that." Once that is said or thought, there is no place to go from there. The French philosopher Rene Descartes is famous for the credo, "I think, therefore I am." Let us step outside the mind/body dualism context of the philosopher's words and rephrase Descartes's famous adage to say this: "I think, therefore you are what I think you are." That is how the ideology of different races has come to be an accepted fact—via projection. Psychologist Nancy McWilliams says that projection is "the mental process by which people attribute to others what is in their own minds."[34] Greek philosophers would use a word, *noeta*, to say, "I think, therefore there is that which I think,"[35] to advance an idea similar to projection. Or to put that same idea in Funk vernacular speech, "It is what it is," depending on what is going on inside *my* head. Do we really believe it is possible to know another person, let alone another entire race, by projection? History seems to indicate it has been attempted many times, but I am arguing that it shouldn't have even been tried.

Allow me a hypothetical. Let us imagine that you live in an apartment on the fourth floor and it is directly across the street from a single-family home. That home has a large porch and from time to time the porch attracts homeless people seeking shelter from the elements. As one would expect, debris piles up over time and that irks the homeowner. One day you are out on your balcony and notice that a lone homeless man is sitting on the porch. Suddenly the front door opens and out comes the enraged homeowner who pours a bucket of water over the homeless man's head. The man lets out a loud shriek and runs down the street.

The facts are these, you clearly saw that the substance was water, and you think you know the feeling because you have experienced water on your body before. However, in this scenario you have no way of knowing

---

33. Saini, *Superior,* 42.

34. McWilliams, "Projection," line 1.

35. Louth, *Origins of Christian Mystical,* xiv.

whether the water poured on the man was scalding hot or ice cold. That is because from that distance water just looks like water. The most direct way to be sure what the man felt would have been to experience it yourself. My point is this: Black and white people are marginally aware of each other's life histories. But even that limited knowledge often lacks any experiential basis. The question becomes, why are some insistent that they are endowed with an ability to recognize what racism looks and feels like without ever having experienced it themselves?

One last example. I have a very close white friend who told me that he was wrongfully arrested, roughed up a bit by the police, and then jailed. He said that it was humiliating and he felt dehumanized, but he never considered going out and lighting stores on fire and destroying property in protest. That was *his* experience and he seemed to be hinting that any reasonable person would react to police misconduct in the same manner. Why did he interpret his experience as being similar in kind and intensity to the type that Black people are tired of withstanding? Their protests were about unarmed youth ending up dead on a city street. Was he a proponent of the belief that all people experience life the same way that has been attributed to the philosopher Aristotle's view of the world?

Possibly, but how about this? White kids are taught a history that consists of the people that look like them being portrayed as heroes and people of valor in most instances. In those historical frames, Black people are seldom presented as heroes or people of valor. As an elementary school kid I loved a television series called the *The Gray Ghost*. The show was about "The Civil War exploits of Confederate cavalry officer John Singleton Mosby, nicknamed the Gray Ghost."[36] Somehow, I was enamored with the military skill and cunning of a man fighting for the right to keep my ancestors enslaved. That is so wrong, but illustrative of the power of a well-framed story. On the other hand, the history that white kids are taught rarely include the histories of people that do not look like them. It is then assumed that Black history is akin to Mick Jagger's phrase found in one of his hits, "useless information." The end result of that is one reason why it is so easy to paint Black people as being so very different. The question for us is why? Malicious intent by educators and/or ignorance by whites in general are often cited as possible reasons. The real reason may not be any

36. IMDb.com, "Gray Ghost," para. 1.

more complex than this quote by T. S. Eliot: "Humankind cannot bear very much reality."[37]

THE FUNK OF IT

If cognitive science is about the brain and how it processes information, then Funk is about the heart and how it processes life. What I know about life as a Black man and musician is the result of my experiences and memories. That is what I meant when I said Funk is an extension of Black history. The realities of racism can be discussed using an objective third-person point of view, but its effects, and the sensations produced by it, can only be experienced in the first person. Saint Augustine drives home this point even more forcefully, saying he could "recall what I am, what I have done, and when and where and how it affected me."[38]

Working in the white church world has frustrated me many times because of the attitudes of some of the leadership. I worked in one church where several people on the staff would not speak to me unless another staff person was present to guilt them into it. Many times some of the people I worked with would walk right past me, look at me, and never say a word. I mentioned it to the staff lead and not only was my perception questioned, word got out that I had a bad attitude. I am 100 percent sure that had I told a white attender what was going on, I would have gotten back a version of, "Oh not him, he is always so nice to me, I just don't believe he is a racist." Many times when I have let it be known that I have felt the sting of racism, some will not respond with empathy. Instead, they will choose confrontation. They will challenge whatever does not line up with their "knowledge" about how Black people are treated. This happens without them realizing that behaving in this way is a mild form of racism by definition. What happens in those setting is that people who have never experienced one iota of racism, want to define the race problem, and then fix it on their terms. That probably won't work, and that is the funk of it.

37. Goodreads.com, "Humankind."

38. Augustine, *Confessions*, 186.

6

BEHAVIORAL

Behavioral science is the study of human actions. In the last chapter we looked at how it is we acquire knowledge. Now we will look at the behaviors that are produced by it. Although the actions we are about to discuss result from a certain amount of intentionality, they can also be uncontrolled reactions to events. In some ways the conclusions that are reached in behavioral sciences mimic recent quantum theory that says "everything in nature has a particle nature and a wave nature, and that the objects behavior only exists as probabilities."[1] So as it is with particles and waves, this chapter assumes that behaviors are probabilities and therefore dynamic. To put that in Funk vocabulary, sometimes as human beings "we just do stuff." That is why, as Cartesian philosopher Richard Watson opined, "behavior is in fact . . . an unreliable indicator of what one believes."[2] That suggests that what we are about to discuss is much more complex than the simple "mental process in, behavioral process out" formula you might assume.

To muddy the water even further there is a neuroscientist and author named Sam Harris, who believes "all of our behavior can be traced to biological events about which we have no conscious knowledge."[3] More from him later, but for now let us agree that mental processes are a very important factor in why we behave the way we do. Even if, as we just discussed in the last chapter, they are not always reliable. One example being that the ideology of racial superiority has been implanted into the Western mind via a long and thorough process of self-deception. Some very bad behavior

1. Lanza and Berman, *Biocentrism,* 56.
2. Watson, *Solipsism,* 69.
3. Harris, *Moral Landscape,* 103.

has followed that mistaken notion of biological difference. Just think, if racist behaviors were only biological responses to certain events that would be a scary place for us to be. This would produce the sheer hopelessness of people not being able to control their racial animus. Given all that, do you believe it is even possible to accurately predict the way people will behave in any given situation? Let us turn to the animal kingdom in search of clues that might be of help in answering that question.

I have owned five pit bull dogs during my life. Well, actually three, because two of them were Staffordshire bull terriers—which are essentially a smaller British version of the popular American breed. Today the American pit bull terrier is considered ferocious and therefore unsuitable for much beyond guard duty. But the Staffordshire bull terrier was once considered so people-friendly and trustworthy that they were used to babysit children; "The Stafford is referred to as the 'nanny dog' in the U.K. because of its ability to function as an able nursemaid for children."[4] It gets even better. A survey conducted by the Eukanuba dog food company found that, "Staffordshire Bull Terriers and West Highland White Terriers have been revealed as the most affectionate and communicative dog breeds . . . Staffies, who are known as the 'waggiest' of breeds, show affection by enjoying a belly rub from their owners."[5] Belly rub, huh? When was the last time you heard the words *pit bull* and *belly rub* in the same sentence—and "waggiest" too?

To be fair, pit bulls can behave in an aggressive manner around other dogs because they, well, think they are supposed to because of what was bred into them. Sadly, many people have erroneously believed that some minority groups have had violence "bred" into them in a similar fashion. They buy into a belief that there are just some races whose innate behaviors are much like that of an American pit bull toward other dogs: violent. Could it be that these feared folks, say a young Black male dressed differently than you, are more desirous of a figurative belly rub than violence, just like a Staffie? Then how would your behavior towards them change?

If you are wondering why I am talking about dogs when the chapter is supposed to be about human behavior, the answer is simple. It is because I want to get to the heart of faulty assumptions that some make about the behavioral tendencies of people whose skin color differs from their own. Have you ever heard the phrase "a foregone conclusion"? It is frequently

4. Petmd.com, "Staffordshire Bull Terrier," para. 3.
5. Walden, "Staffies and Westies," para. 1.

used to mean that what follows is totally accurate. Let us play with that phrase a little to say there are times when the "gone-for conclusion," such as judging a person's actions one way, proved to be totally inaccurate. I am guessing we have all experienced that. Jesus did say this about jumping to conclusions: "In the same way you judge others, you will be judged."[6] That is a challenge to all of us, especially when it comes to race. In the past, judgments made using racial stereotypes have been used to drive wedges between racial groups. Maybe we have allowed negative reputations to be used in their stead similar to what many have done with pit bulls.

IDEOLOGY OF THE SELF—ACCOUNTABLE TO NO ONE

It has been said that "Western thought centers upon the individual as principal unit of value of society."[7] That may be a reasonable conclusion to reach in today's self-driven culture where it is axiomatic that "individuality makes its appearance by being differentiated from other individualities."[8] However, the well-respected British scientist Susan Greenfield argues, "A general message from the literature is that for most people until recently . . . no great emphasis was placed on how differentiated you were from everyone else."[9] That suggests that there have been times in history when it was desirable to consider yourself to be more a part of something, rather than taking steps to be different from it. That certainly is not the case today. We take pride in being a totally unique and independent self.

I would like to suggest that we at least consider an approach to life where the goal of our *being* is to become interlocked with other people, rather than becoming a detached and isolated self. Think about these words from philosopher Martin Buber, who said, "A person makes his appearance by entering into relation with other persons."[10] What I take that to mean is that one finds out who they really are by looking into the mirror of others. Sadly, the Western individualistic mind thinks in terms of relating to other people by comparison—and not so much about relationship with other people via cooperation. As Christian ethicist Jennifer Herdt opined,

6. Matt 7:2, NIV.

7. Andrews, *Practical Theology*, 67.

8. Buber, *I and Thou*, 62.

9. Greenfield, *You and Me*, 16.

10. Buber, *I and Thou*, 62.

"The most vicious of men is he who isolates himself the most . . . The best is he who shares his affection with all his kind."[11] But as Eliezer Berkovits observed, "One can only do this if the self-centeredness of man's vitality is curbed."[12] Asking a self-focused individual in our culture to "deny themselves" as Jesus instructed Christians to do, may simply be asking a bit too much. More about that later.

REMAINING TRUE TO THIS SELF

Today we are moving further and further away from looking to God for answers about what good and bad behavior is. We have become dependent on scientists to provide answers for those types of questions. What if, as Yuval Harari put forward in his best-selling book *Homo Deus*, "Scientists study how the world functions, but there is no scientific method for determining how we should behave"?[13] Then we are left with a state of being that Carlos Santana's band sang about when they shouted, "we ain't got nobody to depend on." Maybe our behaviors are simply manifestations of our "true selves"—once one figures out what or who that is. And we don't need anyone to depend on for anything other than the self. Let us challenge that a bit. What follows is a list of categories that have been used to describe the self that was Jimi Calhoun at different times: Jimi the athlete, Jimi the street brawler, Jimi the musician, Jimi the minister/theologian. So the question comes to mind, which one was my true self? Does a true self even exist? Most of us like to think so because millions of dollars have been spent by people trying to locate a version of themselves that makes them feel content.

We all have the potential to become very different versions of ourselves when the opportunity to do so is present and we are motivated. I know that I have been able to incorporate a variety of very different characteristics into the composite that is present-day Jimi Calhoun. I also know that one of the diagnostic criteria for borderline personality disorder is a shifting self-image, which I take to mean being a chameleon-like person. That is not what I am talking about here. A chameleon will change its color on the spot in order to reflect a change in mood or to deflect investigative attention. Said another way, it changes to avoid being found out. What I am saying is

11. Herdt, *Putting On Virtue,* 299.

12. Berkovits, *God, Man, and History,* 128.

13. Harari, *Homo Deus,* 219.

not like that. It is basically a personalized version of what the Apostle Paul said about himself. And that is he became several different versions of Paul in order to serve God. And his behavior demonstrated that there can be different and better versions of your present self too. As we move on, please keep in mind that a behavioral characteristic is not the same thing as an innate quality. Confusing the two is what has caused so many problems in race relations.

CASE STUDIES FROM THE WORLD OF FUNK

What causes the different behaviors people engage in that some consider to be odd and possibly even bad? Is there a standard or norm to use for comparative purposes? Until very recently the seat of human behavior was believed to be more of a psychological concern than biological. That rested on the assumption that our actions were the result of decisions made inside the psychological aspect of the brain. Then it shifted to the idea that it is actually the brain, meaning the organ itself, that makes decisions for us just like our hearts pump blood. At present there is a return to the brain-controlling body theory because of the development of "brain machines" that can control the behavior of animals. Simply put, many scientists are back to believing that human behavior may stem from how we think about stuff more than a physical reaction to it. Scientists offer a lot of theories and elaborate tests to identify patterns of behavior. Then they develop tests to evaluate and analyze behavioral characteristics, such as the Myers–Briggs, MMPI, and DISC, among others, and that's fine. But please allow me to put the Funk to the idea of personality type identification. I want to present three musical metaphors to illustrate ways that very similar human beings in most of the areas those tests measure can behave differently within a subgroup.

Keep in mind that my personal beliefs are that most of our behaviors stem from nothing more than how it is God wired us. In my opinion, personality typing is important only as far as it helps one understand the behaviors that result from that wiring system. In other words, no causation here. I reached that conclusion as a Funk musician, and now I have the capacity to love a diverse group of personality types just as my faith commands me to. What follows are three consistent patterns of behaviors that I have observed during my musical career. As we look at them, I think it is important to use what I am about to say as a kind of behavioral corrective lens. A common error is made when people make judgments about the behavior of others and then place them in the wrong categorical box. Nothing good comes of arriving at hard-and-fast conclusions about the intrinsic realities of someone's personality based on an incomplete interpretation of observed behavior.

Lead Singer Personality Type: It's All about Me!

Lead singers compose a self-focused, independent, and out-for-themselves personality type that owes nothing to no one. Keith Richards of the Rolling Stones made mention of a lead singer personality type in reference to his, Mick Jagger. These are Keith's words describing what happens when a singer's ego becomes overly inflated: "All lead singers do [get big-headed]. It's a known affliction called LVS. Lead vocalist syndrome."[14] My experience has shown me that since they usually get the most attention from the audience, it does shape their understanding about their place in the band. Problems arising between the lead singer and the rest of the players is almost inevitable because as a band progresses, managers and record company executives like to isolate the person they perceive to be the star for monetary reasons. Typically, the lead singer type will take the music executives up on their offers. They just don't seem to be able to help themselves. I love the lead singers I have worked with, and we are still fast friends. So do not misunderstand me, I do not see it as a fault. What I am talking about is strictly a personality type and the way they see the biz.

Hired Guns: What Do You Have for Me?

This particular personality type is often misunderstood because hired guns seem to have no loyalties. And on the surface they can appear to be heartless musical mercenaries. They are forever sizing up others to see what they can do for them in terms of employment. It took me a while to come to terms with this type. That is because the bands I was in with this type would appear to be doing well. Then boom, without a warning the hired gun type would show up at the gig and quit. What I did not get was that they viewed their involvement in most projects as a straight exchange of money for

14. Richards, *Life*, 454.

services rendered. One drummer I grew up with was like that. He was an extreme case, which makes him a perfect example.

I would run into this guy every few months, and during those in-between times, his whole persona could change dramatically. Once I ran into him on a street in Hollywood. He was decked out in a cowboy hat and extolling the greatness of country music singer George Jones. It was not more than six months later when I ran into him again in pretty much the same area of town. Only this time he had traded in the cowboy garb for spiked hair and cut-off t-shirts that were popular with the emerging punk music scene. What happened? Nothing more sinister than a band offered him more money to play the drums for them and so he changed work clothes. He also jumped into the culture of the new gig with both feet. Self-centered? Disloyal? Nah, just a different business model and one that produced different behavior.

Band Member: It's All About the We!

This personality type is fiercely loyal and dedicated to the group. Actually, this is the one that I can be sure that I am representing accurately. That is because it best describes me and my philosophy throughout my music career. All I ever wanted out of the business side of music was to make a decent living playing music with people I cared about. I actually came close to living that dream on a couple of occasions. Many of my friends outside of my bands viewed me as a bit foolish. They would see me pass on jobs with higher profile artists to remain in these bands that were struggling to make ends meet.

There were other reasons for that, too. My ego never needed to be puffed by being around someone that was above me in rock's pecking order. Moreover, I did not believe that as a bass player I would be so important to someone, like say David Bowie, that he would cancel a world tour be-cause he couldn't get Jimi Calhoun to play bass in his band. That being true, there was never any reason to get a big head about having a certain gig that a thousand other people could and would perform adequately if needed. Please do not misunderstand, I am very grateful to have been a part of headlining acts and playing at large venues, as well as being driven to work in private jets, and recognized on the street, etc. However, the truth is my ego never really needed any of it.

FUNK TYPING'S AFFINITY WITH RACE TYPING

Although the funkified personality types just surveyed stem from my personal observations, they illustrate a tendency we all share, and that is the strong desire to pigeonhole others according to *our* perception of *their* behavior. Isn't that exactly what the ideology of race does, by assigning a person to a category based on observable characteristics? In my case studies from Funk, I assigned musicians to categorical boxes because of the way I judged their personalities. In a racialized world, an entire people group can be assigned to categorical boxes based on nothing more than an extremely thin outer layer of skin. As with the lead singer type from above, Black people are often classified as self-indulgent, undisciplined criminal types. And in keeping with the hired-gun type that asks, "what have you got for me?," many classify Black people as a dependent type that asks of the government much the same question. Fallacies such as these soon become reality in the minds of many. However, observed (fallaciously or not) behavior should never result in the creation of rigid categorical boxes, especially racialized boxes. There is just too much diversity among us for that. Roger Scruton has encouraged us "to treat each other not as mere organisms or things, but as persons who act freely."[15] So, to paraphrase James Brown, "we need to get off that funk," meaning we need to let go of the inclination to view people as "types." And what better time to begin that process than right now?

RACE BY SELF-REPORT

I can say I love you to someone, but if my behavior does not match my words, my self-report is meaningless. I have observed many churches that have sloganized "Love your neighbor," and then not followed it up with behavior consistent with the statement. Here's what I mean by that. How can we say we love others and remain comfortable self-segregating ourselves from the very people we claim to love? Biblical love is about our behavior towards another more than it is about well-crafted slogans and well-meaning intentions. For example, Proverbs 25:21 (NIV) says, "If your enemy is hungry, give him food to eat; if he is thirsty, give him water to drink." On the surface that appears to be actionable love. Love for the other must include actions that are a genuine reflection of a person's intentions.

10. Scruton, *Human Nature*, 140.

In fact, it is safe to say what reflects a person's intentions is behavior. Words are nice but action is better.

Today there are many who expect an automatic acceptance of their self-report concerning their attitude about race. They want their words to be accepted at face value and without scrutiny. I often hear a white person say, "Well, you know I am not a racist." Once that is said it would be bad form for anyone to present examples of behavior that would indicate otherwise. Most often I am confident that the person saying it has no idea that he or she has a different definition for racist behavior than most people on the receiving end would. They probably see racist behavior as an activity similar to physical exercise. A person is either doing it or they are not. When you have a friend with that understanding it is extremely difficult to educate them about racism, even gently. That is because they really do not realize how racism operates and how it affects the everyday lives of Black people. They see poor race relations this way: no observable bad behavior, no racism. Most people in the majority culture evaluate racism as an abstraction, meaning conceptually or as an idea. While most Black people evaluate racism cerebrally as well, but also by the way it wreaks havoc in our lives. There is a major difference in perception and that makes it a challenge to have any type of substantive and productive conversations about race.

FEAR—THE ULTIMATE IMMOBILIZER

In race relations there has been one consistent impediment to progress and that is fear. In fact I would go so far as to say that the idea of race is a fear factory. And what that factory produces is racism. There are many who would suggest that the fear of the unknown is most common, and in some ways, the most debilitating. David Hume is said to have believed that Christianity, and religion in general, was birthed out of a "fear and anxiety about future events."[16] There is a section title in the book *The Culture of Fear* that says "Roosevelt Got It Wrong."[17] What that title is alluding to is the famous quote of President Franklin Roosevelt: "The only thing we have to fear is fear itself."[18] The first sentence after that header in the book reads, "We had better learn to doubt our inflated fears before they destroy us."[19] The author

16. Herdt, *Putting on Virtue*, 315.
17. Glassner, *Culture of Fear*, xxiii.
18. Archives.gov, "FDR's," para. 4.
19. Glassner, *Fear*, xxiii.

then asserts that fear can be beneficial in certain situations, such as alerting one to danger. Then he suggests that it can also have a paralyzing effect when, as often is the case in racial interactions, the only danger present is what is imagined. Let us look at a few of the common fears in our culture.

Fear to Risk

Being there for the other automatically brings to the surface a certain amount of fear. For example, fear of failure, fear of disappointment, fear about whether we can meet the expectation of the other. How about this one: If I give my all will I get back their all? The last one seems like a basic question. The problem is we are not the best judge of what that "all" inside of us is. That is why there are coaches in athletics to bring out what they see and not what the athlete believes. I have always maintained that the best coaches may not be the one with the best strategies, or practice regimens, but the ones who recognize potential. God recognizes the potential in us and has the wisdom and patience to draw it out. And wisdom and patience could be the best tools for overcoming the fear of being open.

Fear to Be Responsible Beyond the Self

Being responsible to another human being is viewed as a burden. One version of the golden rule found in another Abrahamic religion, Islam, reads like this: "You should desire for others what you desire for yourself."[20] The quote is a great example of selfless reciprocity. However, that is not my reason for bringing this up now. The word *desire* is. If we define desire as a longing, then it becomes a very important word. That is because many believe that our unfulfilled longings reveal who we really are. Said in simpler terms, "You are what you pursue." Thomas Hobbes said it this way: "Everything we do is motivated solely by the desire to better our own situations, and satisfy as many of our own, individually considered desires as possible."[21] It is very difficult to convince someone raised in a Hobbesian world view that the kingdom of God is based on a different set of principles.

20. Imamaliquotes.tumblr.com, "Your Savior," line 1.
21. Iep.utm.edu, "Social Contract," para. 4.

THE WORLD OF MICRO-LOVE AND MACRO-HATE

Public outbreaks of racial tension are the aftereffect of years without much positive action taken by those who could actually make a difference. For the most part, people feel that if they are not personally engaged in racist behavior, they feel no connection to "those racists." I agree. That type of person is not culpable, but he or she could be partially responsible. Martin Luther King, Jr. said, "Only goodness can drive out evil and only love can conquer hate."[22] Inherent in that quote is that when love is needed, there is an action required. Doing nothing is not a neutral stance, it is an empowering stance for evil to spread. Without people of good will making the effort to drive out evil in the form of racist behavior at the micro level, racism will not only continue at the macro level, it will also grow. Then it will become even more entrenched as a part of our understanding of what normal behavior is related to race.

People should not stand idly by and watch the centuries-old habit of mistreating Black people continue to happen and simply accept it as just "part of life." Especially people in the church world. What a horrible witness that is. Sadly, that has been the church's history. Please understand, I do not believe the majority of any people group fails to love others because they are callous and cold hearted. Then what is the problem? In church settings it might stem from the abdication of responsibility by leadership to inform people that following Jesus includes altering their behavior, and not just spiritualizing what they are already doing. I believe people of faith are supposed to be those who are willing to lay it all down when they see evil and not downplay it or ignore it. I realize that might be tough to hear, but there is a lot of evidence that it has been God's plan for us since the time of Noah. Let us close out with a look at the Noahide covenant, which many in the Jewish (and Christian) tradition understand to be binding on us all.

According to Genesis, the Noahide laws were seven commands given when God repopulated the earth. They are inclusive of everyone, Jews and Gentiles alike. Regarding human behavior there were six that were negative, meaning don't do: behavior such as idol worship, blasphemy, dietary restrictions, theft, sexual sin, and murder. The seventh calls us to establish courts that enforce laws justly. The key word is *justly*. When people create social systems that begin with practical concerns, the result is often policies that are antithetical to God's plan. That is because it inevitably ends with an

22. King, *Strength to Love*, 42.

unequal justice system in place. The reason for that is that laws are passed for the benefit of the powerful, not the weak. But God does desire just and equal treatment for the weak, whoever the weak may be. And as difficult as this may be to hear, the weak in our country have always been dark-skinned people.

Recently there has been a slew of "how to not be a racist" books that have caught the fancy of Christians worldwide. Unfortunately, many people who have read them seem to have missed the key word in my sentence and that is "be." Obviously, "be" is part of the word *behavior,* making the two terms related. Yet those books appear to have resulted in people focusing more on what it is they think about racism, without ever examining their own behavior. Otegha Uwagba observed that good intentions without behavioral change was inadequate to put a dent in the type of racism operating today. In her book *Whites* she stated that "when it is not their lives or their livelihood or their freedom that's at stake,"[23] that leaves little motivation to make any changes in their behavior. Simply put, people without their own skin in the game view the game quite differently from the actual players. But as Nassim Taleb wrote, "skin in the game is necessary to understand the world,"[24] and I would also suggest, to understand racism too.

THE FUNK OF IT

My experiences growing up as a Black kid forced me to have to create several versions of my "self." I became a racial being that needed a dual passport to survive. While my skin was dark, I had white friends, white bandmates, and crushes on the white girls in my classes. You know, going through the normal phases kids go through on the road to adulthood. Over time I developed a deep love for many kids belonging to the people group that viewed me as inferior and let me know it. When I was young that left me very confused. At one point that confusion turned to a hatred in my heart for the way I was treated on a daily basis.

Please note that the word *hatred* was directed at the treatment I received and not at the people doling it out. That said, during my early years there never seemed to be a let-up. Something seemed to happen daily to remind me of who I was and that I didn't really belong. If it wasn't a comment made under someone's breath, then it was a stare. If it wasn't being

23. Uwagba, *Whites,* 57.
24. Taleb, *Skin,* 3.

followed while shopping, it was a police officer treating me like a criminal during a traffic stop. There was always something. The biggest surprise to you may be that each one of the reminders I just mentioned continue to happen. Every one of them. I am aware some have a very hard time imagining that what was just shared was true and remains true—but sadly it is. That's the funk of it.

7

SOCIOLOGICAL

Seminary professor Norman Gottwald observed, "Society may be described as a group of people sharing a self-sufficient system of action . . . It has to do with patterned relationships among human actors."[1] Sociology can also be defined as "the study of social problems,"[2] and in my lifetime there has been no greater social problem than Black and white race relations. Racism is not really a "problem" because image bearers of God should never be characterized as a "problem." Racism is a relational malfunction that creates social imbalance. For a well-ordered society to exist there must be something that holds it together. We know there are plenty of options out there such as politics, nationalism, self-interest, racial affiliation, as well as religion. But as political scientist Efraim Podoksik noted, "Sociology and its alleged 'laws,' out of which a system is pretentiously constructed . . . cannot do justice to the real nature of social practices."[3] That says to me if racial problems exist, they may be the result of social practices that occur on a daily basis, you know, the little things people do. Poor race relations are not the result of a problem created by the few, but a failure of the many to love.

The authors of the book *When the Ways of Life Collide* suggested that the science of sociology cannot address all of our racial missteps because "what it actually measures—is not obvious on its face."[4] Simply put, many of the components of racism are attitudinal, therefore unobservable. One

1. Gottwald, *Social Justice*, 4.
2. Lexico.com, "Sociology," line 1.
3. Podoksik, *Cambridge Companion to Oakeshott*, 77.
4. Sniderman and Hagendoorn, *When the Ways of Life*, 91.

other reason is that "scientific inquiry involves abstracting."[5] But our social lives are not comprised of abstractions. They are comprised of relationships. This chapter is titled "Sociological" because as theologian Daniel B. Clendenin suggested, "Sociology helps the church community examine itself."[6] And that is fine, but in 2 Corinthians 13 Paul told people *in* the church to examine themselves, and maybe that is something we should consider doing in order to become a racism-free church.

The Cambridge Dictionary defines the word *signification* as follows: "Their bodies are historically coded and permanently marked with significations that forces them into categories they cannot choose."[7] In our culture skin color sends coded messages to people and they are negative. Hans-Georg Gadamer observed that signs function "only because the linkage between the sign and the signified has previously been established."[8] We have a long history of race theory that is woven into every aspect of our social fabric. We got there because many have never made the effort to question the discredited theory that "race is traceable on the body."[9] There are many folks in our churches that genuinely believe the outward sign of skin color is a legitimate path to knowing a person's inner essence.

SIGNS ALL AROUND US

Consider the "street" or colloquial version of signification that I grew up with in my inner city neighborhood. We referred to it simply as "signifying." Signifying meant to playfully point out attributes about someone that forced the person into a particular category. It was a mild form of judgmental labeling disguised as good clean fun. Author Imani Perry stated in *Prophets of the Hood*, "Sam Floyd describes the meaning of Signifyin(g) when applied to the black musical tradition: Signifyin(g) is a way of saying one thing and meaning another, it is a reinterpretation."[10] Commenting in his now classic text *The Signifying Monkey*, Henry Louis Gates wrote, "In relating the black linguistic sign 'Signification' to the standard English sign 'signification' . . . these two 'identical' signifiers, these two homonyms, have

5. Podoksik, *Cambridge Companion to Oakeshott*, 77.

6. Ellul, *Presence of the Kingdom*, xxxiii.

7. Dictionary.cambridge.net, "Signification," para. 2.

8. Gadamer, *Truth and Method*, 154.

9. King et al., *Otherwise Worlds*, 125.

10. Perry, *Prophets of the Hood*, 61.

everything to do with each other, and then again, absolutely nothing."[11] You see when people I knew were signifying on each other they were not doing so from an outsider's perception of "the other." The sign, or signification, of skin color was never the basis for what was thought or said. However, that rarely happens in the way races relate to each other in America. It is always about the color of the skin. Perhaps the following analogy will give more clarity about what I mean.

Imagine you are a white female and you are telling a story about being the only person in an elevator en route to the fourteenth floor of a New York office building. You go on to say that a large Black man entered on the next floor and you knew there were twelve more stories to travel before you would arrive at your lawyer's office. Let us throw in that even the tone of your voice changed when you said the "large Black man" part. What do you think your children or friends listening heard you say? Let's be honest, it was probably fear that was communicated, even though it was not mentioned directly. It is time to develop initiatives designed to "un-signify" the unstated racial meaning in everyday speech that we all are accustomed to hearing. As we move on please keep this in mind: a signifier and the signified are both terms that require meaning affixed to them. What that says colloquially is that a book and its cover are not the same thing, and they should not be judged as such.

THE SCIENTIFIC EYE

As unscientific as street signifyin(g) is, there is one component of it that is strictly scientific. The process of signifyin(g) would fit nicely into the discipline of what has been called "the science of perception." A University of Colorado web page describes that type of science this way: "The brain constructs the experience of reality using sensory information from the outside world combined with internal information from memory, fears, desires, and goals."[12] I understand this to mean, and why I see it as being similar to signifyin(g), is that the materials used to make these assessments come into the brain from outside of our body. Our eyes see something that in turn causes the brain to interpret the "sign." Then our pre-existing understanding helps us make a determination about what we should think

11. Gates, *Signifying Monkey*, 50.
12. Colorado.edu, "Illusion and Reality," para.1.

about what the sign pointed to. For example, a Black male is harmlessly walking towards you and you become fearful. That happens every day.

Neuroscientist Michael Graziano writes that "social neuroscience began in the 1950s."[13] It concluded there can be times when we see something and "signals are sent on to other parts of the brain in a sense telling the rest of the brain,"[14] here comes danger. What is most interesting to me, and germane to our conversation, is that he later adds, "Of all the visual signals that flow through the enormously complex cortical visual systems, we are consciously aware of some signals and not others."[15] Uh oh. Does this mean there are times when people see things and react without analyzing what it is they observed? Psychologist Timothy B. Wilson offers an example. "When we meet somebody for the first time, we pigeonhole them according to their race, gender, or age very quickly, without realizing we are doing it."[16] So some of our social perceptions are made for us without any effort being made on our part. Consider how these types of perceptions may result in problems in our legal system.

I WANT MY COURT TV

What can be misunderstood will be misunderstood. ABC News reported an event that happened in Georgia that garnered national attention. My reason for presenting it to you in this fashion is I want to make sure my emotions do not color my characterization of the events. You see I have been accosted by police walking down a street in running clothes. The officers said the reason for the stop was that I resembled someone who had broken into a house earlier in the day. At the time I worked at the largest church in a small area of Los Angeles. I can reasonably assume that some of the congregation must have driven by and observed me standing on a sidewalk in handcuffs. That humiliation has stayed with me for decades. That said, back to the case in Georgia.

> [Ahmaud] Arbery's family says he was out jogging, while the Mc-Michaels have said they thought he was a burglar, according to the Glynn County police report. Gregory McMichael armed himself with a .357 Magnum and his son grabbed a shotgun after Gregory

13. Graziano, *God, Soul, Mind, Brain*, 111.

14. Graziano, *God, Soul, Mind, Brain*, 111.

15. Graziano, *God, Soul, Mind, Brain*, 119.

16. Wilson, *Strangers*, 53.

McMichael saw Arbery "hauling ass" down the street, the police report said. According to the report, a third man—later identified as a neighbor, William Bryan—tried to block Arbery during the pursuit.[17] Gregory McMichael told police that he thought Arbery was a burglar who had recently been targeting the neighborhood. The McMichaels told police that when they caught up with Arbery, he attacked Travis McMichael, who fired his weapon in self-defense.[18]

One of the sadder parts of the story is that a public records request by a local news agency revealed "there had been just one confirmed burglary in the neighborhood from Jan. 1 to Feb. 23: the theft of a handgun from an unlocked truck parked outside Travis McMichael's house on Jan. 1."[19] The shooter flat-out lied to the investigators at the scene. The question that immediately enters my mind is why would Mr. McMichael make the claim of protecting his neighborhood from multiple burglaries not being privy to how many there actually had been—unless he had a firm expectation that his word would be accepted at face value?

Consider this, a white friend of mine who viewed the video of this incident made note of the fact that the victim's attempt to disarm the person confronting him contributed to his death. Why did he not consider the jogger's right to self-defense? What would you do if two or three armed persons unknown to you were following you down a street? We have no way to know what was said by the assailants, but it is safe to assume something was. This we do know for sure: three armed men were chasing an unarmed jogger and when some physicality ensued, it was characterized as a fight or a struggle. People in America have lived most of their lives believing that Black skin automatically signals danger. That leads some to lean in the direction of siding with the men that did the shooting regardless of the particulars involved. I imagine they picture themselves in a situation where "an angry Black man" is coming after them, and in their mind they would shoot too. All the while they forget that it was the white men who were the ones that were actually angry. To expose the way race plays out in a courtroom, what follows is excerpted testimony from a character witness for Mr. McMichael at trial.

17. Griffith, "Ahmaud Arbery," para. 2.
18. Griffith, "Ahmaud Arbery," para. 3.
19. Griffith, "Ahmaud Arbery," para. 4.

The lawyers for Mr. McMichael told the judge that he had served as a lifeguard and saved many lives, hoping to illustrate what an upstanding citizen he was. Then the questions went to a character witness. On cross examination the prosecutor asked Zachary Lanford, "Do you recall a text exchange between you and the defendant Travis McMichael in which he is discussing shooting a black coon with gold teeth that had a high point 45?"[20] Langford responded, "He was referring to a raccoon."[21] The prosecutor follows up with a tinge of sarcasm asking, "A raccoon with gold teeth and a high point .45 ?"[22] Sticking to his "guns," Lanford said, "It was being facetious."[23] The article noted that in a previous hearing it came out the n-word was a regular part of the defendant's vocabulary.

The point here is that even with his friend being fully aware that Mc-Michael's racial attitudes were on public display, he thought he could sell the "not-really-a-racist-but-a-joker" narrative. Why did he feel that was an option? Did he assume that what goes on behind closed doors stays behind closed doors unless a do-gooder blows the whistle? But Court TV did show this testimony, and this witness used the word "crackhead." Then he added as part of his response, "the raccoon needed Newport cigarettes," which many whites perceive to be smoked disproportionately by Black people. American history is replete with instances where equally outlandish representations were put forward in a courtroom that led to dismissals or outright acquittals of actual perpetrators. While on the other side of the equation, our jails may house many people who were guilty of nothing more than matching the description of one group's stereotype of a criminal.

ALL AROUND THE WORLD

A song popular during my youth said that all around the world rock and roll was here to stay. I want to piggyback on the terminology to say that we are approaching a time when a song needs to be written that says, all around the world the Black and white divide is here to stay. This is why. The other night Julaine and I were watching a TV program about the world's great cities named "Legendary Cities." While taking a break I Googled to see how some of the cities compared in terms of population. I was shocked

20. Henke, "Defense Attorneys," line 12.
21. Henke, "Defense Attorneys," line 13.
22. Henke, "Defense Attorneys," line 14.
23. Henke, "Defense Attorneys," line 15.

to see that Moscow was listed as the largest European city in the world. In school I was drilled to get under the desk in preparation for the nuclear fallout from a bomb dropped by that group of evil people. I still have a flight case in my garage with a sticker on it from a gig I did in 1980 for the organization Alliance for Survival, protesting the ongoing Russian nuclear threat. And now they are nothing more than a variety of Europeans? How did that happen? What I want us to look at right now is not European whiteness, but Blackness that comes in the form of two Russians.

I am reading an excellent biography titled *Soul to Soul: A Black Russian Woman's Search for Her Roots*. It tells the story of a woman torn between completely different social identities. The book is approximately three hundred pages of tragedy and triumph, racism, and acceptance. It highlights the determination it took for her to not only overcome, but to succeed.

The book opens with Yelena Khanga recalling her early years of having been born a Black person in Russia. The opening sentences are recollections of her hearing her mother belting out songs, "in a low voice that combines the smoky intonations of a black American blues singer with her classical Russian accent."[24] She goes on to say, "I love the classical melodies my mama plays, with verses by Pushkin . . . One thing every Russian schoolchild knows is that our country's greatest poet is descended from blacks—just like Mama and me."[25] As I read those words I looked back on my own schooling knowing that nothing Black outside of slavery was ever mentioned. Even then, the focus was on the heroic efforts of the white people freeing the slaves, and not the reprehensible behavior that caused the problem in the first place. Our schooling was so poor in that regard that my friend Clifford used to say, "They didn't invent Black people until 1955" when the civil rights movement began making headlines. That was because there was hardly ever any mention of us in the history books or the news unless it could be tied to crime.

Khanga's book closes by following a wonderfully written story that weaves its way through multiple family trees and continents of residence. Then to her facing the realties about the way race has affected her life—and how she can never really be "at home" any place but within her own skin. She records the following words of lament voiced by her mom after receiving her American passport: "There are emigres here [in America] who don't have a good thing to say about Russia . . . but I don't understand them

24. Khanga and Jacoby, *Soul to Soul*, 1.
25. Khanga and Jacoby, *Soul to Soul*, 1.

. . . My language, my culture, a huge part of my thoughts are Russian. But I feel at ease in America too."[26] Then Khanga concludes with a sentence that is also true of every Black person living in America whether or not they ever leave its shores. "I am a Russian citizen but, like my mother, I expect to belong to both worlds for the rest of my life."[27] If you are Black in America you must live as an African without a knowledge of Africa—and you must also view the world as though you are of European descent. It is hard to get along otherwise.

The second "Black Russian" I want to mention was a man named Frederick Thomas. His father was a freed slave who was murdered, prompting Thomas to leave America. "Seeking greater freedom, he traveled to London, then crisscrossed Europe—and in a highly unusual choice for a black American at the time—went to Russia."[28] The story goes on to tell a tale of hardship and perseverance. Thomas eventually becomes extremely successful as an entrepreneur and entertainer just before the Bolshevik revolution. What I found fascinating was that a person commenting on the book said it was remarkable that an African American could leave his homeland, travel to an unknown land, and then make a life for himself. I wondered why, if Thomas's father had been an African slave, and he had only lived on US soil for a short while, why would anyone assume that Thomas perceived America to be his "homeland"? What is it that must be in place, in strictly a sociological sense, for a section of the earth to be considered one's homeland anyway? Let us look at how unstable the idea of belonging based on where one's mother happens to be when she gives birth is. British author and historian Orlando Figes cites Fyodor Dostoevsky as having said:

> When we turn to Asia, with our new view of her, something of the same sort may happen to us as happened to Europe when America was discovered. For, in truth, Asia for us is that same America which we still have not discovered. With our push towards Asia we will have a renewed upsurge of spirit and strength . . . In Europe we were hangers-on and slaves, while in Asia we shall be the masters. In Europe we were Tatars, while in Asia we can be Europeans.[29]

The American narrative seems to be that people of Western European descent have never engaged in behaviors that led to violence unless they

26. Khanga and Jacoby, *Soul to Soul*, 302.
27. Khanga and Jacoby, *Soul to Soul*, 302.
28. Amazon.com, *Black Russian*, para. 2.
29. Figes, "Russia and Europe," sec. 3, para. 3.

were forced to it. That was the viewpoint of many in spite of Europe's collective history of glamorizing warrior culture with all its violence. In fact there have been a plethora of films today that portray a warrior as being honorable and noble. From the Viking marauders, to the crusading invaders, to the age of discovery that resulted in the violent colonization of most of the globe, killing people was the maker of heroes. If my characterization caused you to think, "Wait a minute, that's not right," please consider these statistics: "Although Europe represents only about 8 percent of the planet's landmass, from 1492 to 1914, Europeans conquered or colonized more than 80 percent of the entire world."[30] Do you think they were invited in or fought their way in? Moreover, it is probably wise for you to remember that many histories are just one version of what actually occurred and nothing more. With that in mind, let us now look a little closer at our English roots.

OUR ENGLISH ROOTS: THE FRUIT OF RELIGIOUS SIGNIFICATION

An English politician named William Wilberforce was an important figure in the fight against African chattel slavery. Because of his indefatigable spirit fighting against the "legal" transatlantic slave trade he was nicknamed "A Hero for Humanity." However, he was not alone in those efforts. There was a Scottish man named Zachary Macaulay who was certainly less famous than Mr. Wilberforce, but might have been equally important in the fight to abolish the practice of slavery. Macaulay spent time on a slave ship traveling from Sierra Leone to Jamaica. He observed, "Anyone likely to cause trouble were shackled in the hold, with the most troublesome not only chained at the wrists and ankles only but also by the neck."[31]

The prospects of those previously free Africans, "legally" transported from their homeland to British colonies abroad were remembered this way by Macaulay: "Their cup is full of pure unmingled sorrow, the bitterness of which is unalloyed by almost a single ray of hope."[32] That illustrates perfectly the way inhumane treatment for an entire race of people can be overlooked by another because it was represented as being legal. That in turn should encourage you to consider whether or not there are inhumane

30. Stoller-Conrad, "Why Did Western Europe," para. 1.
31. Cook, *Macaulay,* 65.
32. Cook, *Macaulay,* 66.

and immoral activities being carried out on our streets right now. Have we just come to accept them as part of life because they are legal?

Consider something else about laws that are created in order to regulate societies. The previous example alone should be a clear illustration of harm done by bad laws. But there is one other example that is even worse. A slave trader on African soil wanted the enslaved people who were "granted" freedom on American soil returned to him, and it was noted that "technically he was in the right."[33] That was because according to the British, "no law had yet been passed forbidding the trade."[34] In my view that was convoluted, as well as an example of how people can become blind to injustice by some very bad laws. I see many people condoning evil as long as they can point to an existing law to support their position, as though the laws written by the leaders of a country are equal to those written by God.

JUST OBEY THE LAW

Okay, but who drafted the laws and for what purpose? Allow me to share another example that might be even more contradictory related to the crafting of "just" laws. This occurred during the time when the British were "legally" transporting African people to what is now the United States. When the British lost the Revolutionary War, they transported most of the recently freed slaves (who had fought for them) to Nova Scotia rather than England. When that arrangement did not work out they transported them "home" to the African continent. There was one fatal flaw in their reasoning. How did the British have property rights to the land on which Sierra Leone was founded? Zachary Macaulay biographer Faith Cook made the following observation about the irony in the freedoms given to formerly enslaved Africans upon their arrival on the continent that originally spawned them.

> A core of settlers, mainly some who had come from Nova Scotia, were always on the look-out for causes of dissatisfaction. They disliked the judicial system set up by Macaulay and wished to appoint men of their own choosing to positions of authority. A yet more contentious issue igniting their fury concerned their demand to own the freehold of the land on which their homes were built.[35]

33. Cook, *Macaulay,* 88.
34. Cook, *Macaulay,* 88.
35. Cook, *Macaulay,* 99.

The question for us at this point is who appointed whom to manage anyone without their consent or willingness? The Europeans granted for themselves the right to control the behavior of people from other ethnic groups. They assumed that African soil was their property to give or keep. And they saw no problem transporting people they didn't even know thousands of miles to where three different nation-states now exist. That requires some chutzpah! There are some people who believe it is wrong to break any law, period. How many of God's laws do you reckon were violated by what you just read? We need to remember that all civil laws were initially crafted to benefit one specific group and to support one type of social arrangement. Quite often the morality of those laws were of secondary importance.

My broader point concerning all of this is not so much about the laws themselves, but about the attitudes of the people who made them. What was the mind-set of the people who granted themselves the right to forcibly move halfway around the globe another group of people that had not attacked them, and who bore them no hostility? Secondly, even when the British decided to do the right thing and "free" them, they did so in such a way that the remedy did not inconvenience themselves. Sure, there was the decision to move "their" former enslaved people to North Africa. But they moved them to land that was really not theirs to dole out. "Archaeological findings show that Sierra Leone has been inhabited for thousands of years."[36] One of the rationales for colonization was that the land was uninhabited. Try to imagine the story they had to tell themselves to justify that undertaking knowing that wasn't true. The stories we tell ourselves can make a wrong seem right. The sadder part is that all the uprooted Africans ever wanted was that the pre-Revolutionary War rhetoric of "natural rights, liberty, and the promise of equality"[37] be applied to them too. What needs to be fully understood is that there are many people of African descent today who believe they are still waiting for those promises to materialize.

THE FUNK OF IT

Many times I have voiced frustration at the way I have been treated by law enforcement, and the laws police used to give themselves permission to do it. Some people seem to have a conditioned response that if I would just obey the law there would be no problem. What is so funky about this is,

36. Britannica.com, "Sierra Leone," para. 3.
37. Berlin, *Making of African America*, 97.

I am fearful of the police on the streets of a city where I pay thousands of dollars in taxes, and I do obey the law. I drive in constant fear that I will be humiliated if not killed and that is a funky way to have to live. When I am out at night my wife worries whether or not I will make it home. That is a funky way for her to live too and it shouldn't be happening. And it is all because of race.

It is time that people come to the realization that some of our social problems may be rooted in the laws themselves. For example, Julaine and I watched an English television series titled *Island at War*. It was based on the German occupation during World War II of the Channel Islands located off the coast of France. Prior to the war it had been part of the British Isles, but the English decided to abandon it when hostilities began. The town in the film had its own police force before the invasion and that is what caused the tension. What follows will illustrate my point that every law is not sacrosanct just because it is called the law. Laws can be extremely unjust.

Once the Germans arrived there was tension between the local police captain and the German officers. In one scene the German officer explained to the police captain that he should obey the law. The officer reminded him that those were German laws and not the laws that the Islanders lived by before the occupation. I put it to you now, which laws were "right"—the ones in place before it was invaded, or the German laws because they were now the people in power? If you sided with the Islanders, then you are admitting that some laws crafted by one group can be oppressive over another. If you sided with the Germans, then you are admitting that "law and order" is not always a matter of justice but of power.

The reality is this. I have experienced both scenarios as a Black man living under a legal system that was not originally designed with my people group's best interests in mind. Then being policed by people who are given charge to enforce laws in any way they see fit. Maybe some of those laws are as unjust as the ones the Germans imposed on the English. If so, that is really a funky way to treat people. Know this, I have been beaten, had guns pulled on me, and verbally humiliated by police several times. The vast majority of those incidents occurred when I was guilty of nothing other than being Black. You may choose to not believe me, or you may not like hearing it, but that is the truth of it. If you are a person who desires to help move the racial reconciliation conversation forward in a meaningful way—then it will require you to open your mind and heart to the histories and experiences of the other *before* any conversation begins. That is the Funk of it.

Part Three

BEING

"Where questions of culture become irrelevant . . ."
—ANTONY GROMELY

8

THE POLITICS OF BEING

There are many that would argue, as Catholic scholar John Meier has, that "a human being only becomes fully human by entering into dynamic relationships of friendships, love, enmity and hate, control, subordination and collaboration with other humans."[1] What would you imagine the best instrument would be to facilitate that many intense human social pursuits? Since the American and French revolutions, people in the West have seemed to take it for granted that politics is far and away the best choice. Politics are a combination of rules, requirements, and legal obligations that provide a framework designed to regulate the social interactions of citizens. The form of politics that has grown out of those conflicts has been one of a centralized authority actively supporting, sanctioning, or validating the dynamic relationships spoken of by Meier. However, the politics of being is the result of an eternal authority who actively invites all of us into a dynamic relationship with a political party that can never be voted out.

Historian Brad Gregory noted that during the period when secular politics was separating itself from religion some were of the opinion that, "Left to their own choices, Americans might choose not to clothe the naked, for example, or not to feed the hungry, or to care for the sick."[2] Previously those duties had been the responsibility of the church because it was understood that Jesus had called the people of God to be directly involved in carrying them out. In our society, many who identify as today's people of God do not view those things as part of their Christian duty but a function

1. Meier, *Marginal Jew*, 2.
2. Gregory, *Unintended Reformation*, 172.

of the state. They believe that being free in Christ actually means being "free to live for their own enjoyment and pleasures . . . to pursue their desires while ignoring whomever they choose to ignore."[3] That perspective has not only fueled racism, but it has also kept people looking in the direction of government more than God for their security. Today we seem to be at a place where civic duty is accepted as a necessary part of life, but any mention of Christian duty is summarily rejected because it is viewed as onerous and legalistic.

In a kingdom of God-centered political understanding, rather than seeking permission from the state to act, people opt in—meaning their involvement is unregulated and voluntary. Secular governments roll on the rails of coercion and restriction, be it by taxation, regulation, or through licensure that allows a person to work in their chosen profession, etc. There are so many people invested in that form of politics that it would be very difficult for them to imagine a society without a strong central government. It is taken for granted that a government has the ability to solve any and every problem, whether it is labeled democratic, socialist, authoritarian, or any other form. The politics of being assumes that any attempt to unify people via a centrally planned legal system is doomed to fail. For some reason that still baffles me, even people of faith have come to simply accept the premise that a society cannot function independent of a group of central planners.

I have a close friend who often recalls a humorous incident from her college days. She and a group of friends decided to have a go at communal living. They drew up a set of rules and made a kind of a social contract that each person would meet the agreed-upon requirements. As time passed one person repeatedly failed to take their turn at washing dishes. That person's slothful behavior went on for awhile until the others became frustrated. Eventually the experiment failed. Whenever my friend tells the story it is always with warmth and a smile—evidencing that if it wasn't a pleasant experience, at least it created a good memory. And it also ended with her having one takeaway embedded in her mind, and that was that communism doesn't work unless everyone does their fair share. Maybe the problem was not located in the word *share* but *fair*? Nevertheless, if communism is one of those forms of government that doesn't work, then maybe the others from our list will not either.

3. Gregory, *Unintended Reformation*, 173.

POLITICAL THEORY À LA THE NBA

I know you could be wondering, what do basketball and politics have in common? Let me explain. I played tons of organized basketball as a kid. I was a gym rat all through middle school, meaning I was in my school's gym working on my game almost as many hours as it was open. It would not be unusual for me to spend four to six hours straight playing pick-up games. When teams compete in the NBA, professional referees are hired to monitor the game to make sure the rules are followed. That is not the case in the pick-up games that happen in parks and gyms across America. Over time athletes who play in pick-up games come to play by the rules of an unstated rule book that everybody just sort of knows. My point here is that, unlike my friend's college experience, basketball weekend warriors across the globe have proven that it is at least possible for human beings to self-regulate.

STATE YOUR CASE

Terry Eagleton, in *The Idea of Culture*, said, "In a civil society, individuals live in a state of chronic antagonism, driven by opposing interests; but the state is that transcendent realm in which these divisions can harmoniously be reconciled."[4] That suggests that unlike basketball players with competing interests who are able to develop the skill necessary to self-regulate, our society needs a referee, the state, for the game of life to be played fairly. One of the United States' founding documents suggests that there are three rights that are given by God, our referee, which the state was created to protect. They are life, liberty, and the pursuit of happiness. Uh oh. Will not 200 million or more adults pursuing their own version of happiness lead us right back to Eagleton's conclusion? Is it possible the majority of us have just come to accept that it is not possible for societal health to exist unless a strong central government exists right alongside it?

POLITICAL HEALTH INSURANCE

I recently changed my medical insurance company and just this week I received a letter that outlined my rights and responsibilities. As I was reading them a thought crossed my mind. There seemed to be a word missing

4. Eagleton, *Idea of Culture*, 6.

and that word was *duties*. The letter detailed what I could expect from the medical professionals in the event I needed them. It also explained what financial responsibilities I would assume once I engaged them, etc. What was missing was what I was supposed to do between the start date of my policy and whenever it was that I suffered an illness. Did I have a duty to watch my diet and exercise in order to stay as healthy as possible, or was my health their job?

My older brother was in the Cub Scouts. I can recall him reciting an oath that said, "On my honor I will do my best to do my duty to God and my country and to obey the Scout Law."[5] Inherent in that motto is the recognition that any organization, which a political system is, will run smoothly only if the people involved observe a duty to do their part. The failure of everyone involved to do their duty is what doomed my friend's experience in communal living. The thing is this, no political system can succeed unless people live up to certain responsibilities. In our form of governance, the state coerces people to do their part, but in the kingdom of God, the leader attempts to love you into fulfilling your duty.

COMMUNITAS: THE GIFT OF GOD FOR THE PEOPLE OF GOD

Victor Turner was a British anthropologist known for developing the concept of "liminality . . . and for coining the term 'communitas.'"[6] Turner postulated that the secular and sacred were in a constant state of juxtaposing and alternating, but seems to have settled on seeing them joined in a spirit of communitas. The word *communitas* refers to a system of organization where people choose to live with, and for, each other in pursuit of the well-being of all. Communitas is then a community of the narrowly focused, if you will. In the Scriptures Jesus is not only characterized as our high priest but also the King of all Kings. Most of us have never lived under the rule of a monarch and so it should be stated that a kingship is a political office by definition. Remember that monarchs were most often members of the tribe over which they ruled. That means they were capable of being loyal to the tribe and their political responsibilities at the same time. At that point, deciding which of the two takes priority over the other would have been the question. We often face a similar choice, don't we? Deciding between our

5. Scoutingwire.org, "Cub Scout Motto."
6. Newworldencyclopedia.org, "Victor Turner," para. 1.

tribe, all of humanity—or our politics that consists of one small segment of that humanity.

Graham Ward wrote that secular politics "works out its ideology, its metaphysics of physical and political embodiment through various state-informed practices acting through state-related institutions."[7] Ward goes on to list some of those institutions: "schools, hospitals, universities, religious bodies supportive of state policy, the army, the police force, the courts, and so forth."[8] Now reread the names of the institutions where kingdom principles could be lived out, such as schools, police forces, courts—and you have found the hope-filled process of governance that the politics of being could produce. James Hunter observed, "Politics subsume the public spaces so much so that they become conflated . . . So instead of the political realm being seen as one part of the public life, all of public life is reduced to the political."[9] Politics then becomes all-powerful, or to borrow Graeme Nicholson's term, a "hyper-entity"[10] whose tentacles invade every facet of our daily lives, occupying the very space that Christians should reserve for God.

For that reason, it is easy to be confused about where Christians should place their trust—in a politician or in God. That dichotomy can negate the progress we might have made towards achieving the social cohesion discussed in the previous chapter. That is because "human beings unhappily possess an inbred proclivity to mix ignorance of themselves with arrogance towards others."[11] The politics of being does not seek to create a new world order, only a different way of organizing the old. It creates a world order that is free of judgments about one's job, race, physical limitations, or any of the other criteria people use to justify looking down on an outsider.

DIGNITY IN DIFFERENCE

Jesus has warned us not to go down the road of judgementalism by saying, "In the same way you judge others, you will be judged, and with the measure you use, it will be measured to you."[12] The politics of being has no

7. Ward, *Politics of Discipleship,* 236.

8. Ward, *Politics of Discipleship,* 236.

9. Hunter, *To Change the World,* 105.

10. Nicholson, *Justifying Our Existence,* 131.

11. Stassen and Gushee, *Kingdom Ethics,* 178.

12. Matt 7:2, NIV.

place for "otherizing" in its platform because it is built on the idea of not just liberty for all, but also dignity for all. We have left it to our politicians to make decisions about how much liberty each citizen deserves and we just accept it as something the state has a right to give or take away.

Consider for a moment how the famous Miranda warning is worded. In the US when a law enforcement agent is in the process of taking away one's liberty by arresting them, the suspect is given a "warning." Actually, it is a statement apprising them of their "rights." It usually goes as follows, "You have the right to remain silent but anything you say can, and will, be used against you in a court of law. You have the right to an attorney and if you cannot afford an attorney, one will be appointed for you." My point is this. Showing people being Mirandized on countless television programs and movie screens only reinforces the idea that human rights come from the state.

It is inevitable that our freedom will be in the hands of others to a certain degree, things such as safety, social status among others—but our human dignity should never be. In our society we have just taken it for granted that, as Ron Highfield wrote, "Dignity, like worth, comes in degrees . . . People in authority are more deserving of deference and honor than those under them."[13] Pardon my funk, but that's jive! God's kingdom is built on the idea that dignity is something that each of us is expected to see in the other, and it should never be taken away from them. That is one of the major differences between the organizing principles of secular politics and kingdom politics. In the politics of being it is our responsibility to engage the other by respecting the dignity that God placed in them. This idea supersedes whatever political structures are put in place by us. As Donna Hicks once said about the way dignity is processed, "It comes with the recognition and acceptance of the value and vulnerability of all living things."[14] And let us not forget that John 1:3 clearly states, "Through him all things were made; without him nothing was made that has been made."[15] If God embedded human dignity in us, it can't be taken away by another.

13. Highfield, *God*, 96.
14. Hicks, *Dignity*, 1.
15. John 1:3, NIV.

THE THANG

In classical Greek the word *logos* can be translated to mean, "An eternal and unchanging truth present from the time of creation."[16] There was a word circulating at the beginning of my career playing Funk that was similar to Logos in elasticity and meaning, and that was the word *thang*. One could use it in a variety of ways. Obviously, a thing is a thang, but then an idea is a thang too, and as with the word *logos*, it was descriptive of an eternal truth. If someone wanted to use the word to express a solid verifiable truth they would say, "Ain't nothing but a thang." The great Jewish sage Maimonides, who lived from 1135–1204, meaning way before the Republican or Democratic parties existed, wrote, "Man is political by nature and that it is his nature to live in a society."[17] The fact that Maimonides viewed human beings as having a political bent wired into them "ain't nothing but a thang," or in today's vernacular speech, "true that."

If politics are in fact a thang in the sense they are part of our reality, then politics should have as its mandate social well-being. And that mandate should be in force regardless of the direction a country takes following an election. That is why I am in full agreement with the following statement by Mark Lila: "Biblical political theology is theocentric . . . It begins with God, his word, and above all else his authority . . . There is no genuine knowledge of man without knowledge of God."[18] Politicians that are theocentric recognize that all politics should ultimately be an extension of God's will, and that will is certainly not one of procuring power as its only end.

There is something else that distinguishes theocentric politics from other versions. We are used to seeing politics as a bifurcation, with its adherents believing in the existence of a private sector and civic sector in our society. That idea then leads to the conclusion that every human within a society is entitled to a private life and a public life. That understanding in turn spills over into what we believe it means to be a person of faith. Today we believe it to be axiomatic that each person has a private expression of faith, and also a public version. It is likely that living out faith in that manner has contributed to churches being labeled as places full of hypocrites. When it comes to the politics of being, there really is no way to separate the private from the communal without weakening one of them. The Iona

---

16. Pbs.org, "Logos," para. 1.
17. Weiss and Butterworth, *Ethical Writings,* 134.
18. Lilla, *Stillborn God,* 66.

Community that Julaine and I are associated with believes that life encompasses faith and politics, and for us that is a good way to live.

COUNT IT ALL JOY

In order to strengthen the disciples' faith, Paul and Barnabas told them, "We must go through many hardships to enter the kingdom of God."[19] Kingdom ethics are not always easy to live out, but God promises the end result will be worth any discomfort involved. What holds us back? Not a hard heart but a fearful one. It is fear that makes a social justice message controversial in so many churches. People who are fearful and intolerant of other races may be that way because they believe it leads to nothing more than their rights and preferences being trampled on. They are positive that only discomfort will come of them being in close proximity to people of other races because *they* dress funny, *they* eat different food, and *their* skin color is not what I am used to seeing every day. The list goes on.

Think about this: "When one group of people fails to do what another group of people believes they should do—still more, when they actually do what is what the other group believes that they should not do,"[20]—it can reaffirm the predisposed notion that toleration of the other is a very bad idea. Then the belief that "social distancing" is a better option than engagement comes into play. I once heard a person say after 9/11 that people in America had better learn to check our fears at the door before they destroy us. That is very true in race relations too.

A STATE OF BEING

Let us use the word *state* as a double entendre. First as a condition of being, such as the way we share a "status" report on the popular social media platform Facebook. Second as a label for a governing body in which one's being is situated. In the West the majority of us live in some form of a liberal democracy. The roots of the democratic impulse date as far back as the ancient Greeks but came into focus for us through people like John Locke and Jean Jacques Rousseau. Locke argued that "government should be

19. Acts 14:22, NIV.
20. Sniderman and Hagendoorn, *When Ways of Life*, 20.

limited to securing [protecting] life and property of its citizens."[21] Rousseau developed the concept of a social contract, believing that out of self-interest free and equal citizens would eventually land on the best form of political order—or government—by agreement between those governed. However, democracy does not automatically guarantee freedom or equality for everyone. As Rabbi Jonathan Sacks observed, "Liberal democracy is about togetherness-in-difference, and we begin to lose it [social cohesion] when we notice the difference but forget the togetherness."[22] In spite of many years of rhetoric coming from politicians, skin color continues to be the difference noticed first and noticed most, making it the number one impediment to that democratic ideal being realized.

I can see how theologians of the past could have looked to Ephesians 4:11 to logically conclude that "God had given everyone his or her place."[23] That passage says that in establishing order in the early church Jesus said "some were to be apostles, others prophets, others evangelists, and others pastors and teachers." What is interesting here is, although the Bible did not rank those giftings, it didn't take long for our church culture to do it. We don't just have well-defined roles, we have well-defined ranks of ministry importance. Maybe it is just our nature to establish a pecking order whenever we structure a social grouping. Alain de Botton noted that Aristotle reached the conclusion back in 350 BC that, "It is clear some men are by nature free, and others by nature slave [lower class], and for the latter slavery is both expedient and right."[24] That quote relies on someone making an assessment about what types of human nature belongs where, doesn't it? The lead vocalist juxtaposed with a side man from an earlier chapter illustrates that may not be the best way to organize a band or a society.

The politics of being is grounded in social interactions that result from assumed responsibilities and not a set of requirements handed down by a distant and impersonal government, as those concocted by humans frequently are. The kind of social interaction under discussion here is a positive act. Rules by a government are negative in nature because they inform people what they must not do. Many of the "enticements" governments use to bring people together can be well-intentioned but haphazardly executed. Love is the one problem-solver that never fails. I can be confident of that

21. Moseley, "John Locke," para. 2.

22. Sacks, *Home We Build Together*, 11.

23. Eph 4:11, NTE.

24. De Botton, *Status Anxiety*, 28.

because it was the solution put in place before the world as we know it even started.

THE FUNK OF IT

I was on the board of a non-profit organization whose focus was lobbying churches to be more inclusive of people classified as disabled. One day we were discussing the difficulties that surface when trying to persuade a pastor, an organization, or even a government to alter their perspectives about people living on the margins of society. People in the mainstream of any society can simply live their lives without needing to give much thought about how those at the bottom live, or even why they are there for that matter. In this particular moment a fellow board member quizzed me about what kind of political activities I was involved in to effect change. My answer of none not only startled her but made her angry. She then went on to say that she could never support a clergyperson that was not politically active.

The truth is I really am politically active, just not the type found in the local or national politics that stem from systems created by people. That has been hard for a majority of people here in the US to wrap their heads around. Frankly, there are some who are so committed to their brand of political idealism as being the pinnacle of human endeavor that they cannot imagine how another person could not view it as such. What happens is that if I appear to side with a governmental policy that leads to the most freedom, that will be construed by some to mean that I am a conservative Republican or Libertarian "type." However, if I side with a policy that calls for social responsibility, I am often labeled as a liberal Democratic "type" and a proponent of the social gospel. The truth is I am neither of them, but I am very much a Black type. That means that I highly value freedom. The reason for that is this. My entire life has been spent without ever enjoying the amount of freedom I have had to stand by and watch my white fellow citizens enjoy. As difficult as that may be for some of you to hear, that is the Funk of it!

9

THE ECONOMICS OF BEING

The Encyclopedia Britannica describes an economic system as "any of the ways in which humankind has arranged for its material provisioning . . . corresponding to the many cultural arrangements that have characterized human society."[1] We have just finished looking at politics, and most of us understand that the political realm functions in terms of laws and restrictions. That is evidenced by the fact that whenever the word *justice* is brought up, most of us picture the police, a court of law, or whichever type of legislative body is in place where we live. What picture comes to mind when the concept of economic justice, or injustice, is discussed? Where did the criteria used to decide who is deserving of what in our society originate? Tom Nelson said, "Economic life is messy and imperfect because we live in the context of broken neighbors and broken neighborhoods."[2]

My band named the Project used to perform a Funk song titled "My Money is Funny" to alert the audience that an intermission was about to take place. What we meant was that a person didn't have much money, and when someone's money was "funny" they could not do much. Do you remember the lyrics from Clifford's lament that wondered why there were those that had more than they needed, while others were unable to get what they needed? Allow me to reverse the order of the words in our intermission song. That would lead us to words used in the title "Funny Money," which is a satire written by Ray Cooney. The play was about a man who found a large sum of money in a briefcase and decided to keep it, only to have his life turned upside down because of a lack of experience in "having

1. Heilbroner and Boettke, "Economic system," para.1.
2. Nelson, *Economics*, 71.

money." Our reversed word order could also illustrate the difference in how money affects people. A lack results in limited opportunity and despair, while too much can result in confused priorities.

What is valued in the kingdom of God has very little to do with finance because it is spiritual. Global economics are transactional and usually end with the exchange of something tangible. The economics of the kingdom are experiential and what is exchanged is rarely visible. Put another way, there is a difference between the price of goods, and who has access to the means to acquire the goods under discussion. I believe history has shown us that there have been times when economics have been weaponized to maintain the privileged position of the few over the many. For example, there was a time in England's history when farming went from being a shared or communal endeavor, to one of for-profit, market-based competition. Peter Ackroyd recalls, "The larger farmers wished to sell their produce to the rising populations of the towns and cities; the smaller farmers were reduced to subsistence agriculture."[3] Economics became more a matter of how the markets were performing than one of justice. Or was all of that just about how times change and not everyone changes with them? Ackroyd offered an intriguing observation about the process involved. "So it is with historical change . . . It proceeds over many decades, and many centuries, before becoming irrevocable."[4]

During my touring days it was not unusual for record companies to purchase concert tickets at the venues where their acts performed. This was done to make it appear their acts were more popular than they really were. What that practice did was create an artificial market for the band, with the hope that genuine sales would eventually replace the hype. In that scenario it was perceived that everybody won. Obviously, that was not a foolproof business plan. More often than not the record companies had to write off enormous sums because concert attendance does not always translate to record sales. In *Zen and the Art of Funk Capitalism*, Philip Karun suggests that there are times when "markets are artificially created by democratic governments to re-engineer incentives."[5] That happens when people are coerced into believing they should purchase a product or service in order to benefit society. In the system called kingdom economics there are incentives attached as well. However, those incentives are not found in

3. Ackroyd, *Tudors*, 23.

4. Ackroyd, *Tudors*, 22.

5. Karun, *Zen and the Art of Funk Capitalism*, 29.

the questionable practices of show business people—nor are they found in government intervention. They are situated in a strong desire to see peace and justice reign. These completely different understandings of basic economic theory can be at odds with each other and oftentimes are.

STRANGERS

Numbers 15:15 reads, "The community is to have the same rules for you and for the foreigner residing among you; this is a lasting ordinance for the generations to come. You and the foreigner shall be the same before the Lord."[6] Why is this concept of justice for the outsider ignored, or if not ignored, so difficult to live out? A good place to start would be deciding who is and who is not a foreigner. In our context we are not only talking about the person from a far-off nation-state or an immigrant. We are talking about the person from outside of your particular tribe who you believe to be strange, meaning unusual, curious, odd, weird, or a host of other negatives. Let us be honest, some of those words may run through your mind when you observe someone from that "other race" doing certain things.

Rabbi Sacks offers two very helpful insights that can put us on the road to answering our questions about who is a brother and who is a stranger. This will help us to better understand the economy of the kingdom in the Black and white of it. Sacks first writes, "We encounter God in the face of a stranger . . . God creates difference; therefore, it is in one-who-is-different that we meet God."[7] Sacks writes second, "The knowledge that we are strangers teaches us to reach beyond the boundary of us and extend friendship and reciprocity to them. The knowledge, too, that the earth is not ours, that we are temporary residents."[8] The rabbi's perspectives have really helped me keep a kingdom perspective on the best way to view the stranger in relationship to their place in the world. They deserve having their hopes and dreams realized as much as anyone else.

Psalm 146

He is the Maker of heaven and earth,

6. Num 15:15, NIV.
7. Sacks, "Dignity of Difference," para. 8.
8. Sacks, "Dignity of Difference," para. 9.

the sea, and everything in them
he remains faithful forever.
He upholds the cause of the oppressed
and gives food to the hungry.
The Lord sets prisoners free,
the Lord gives sight to the blind,
the Lord lifts up those who are bowed down,
the Lord loves the righteous.
The Lord watches over the foreigner.[9]

Who were these biblical strangers? UCLA Professor Yona Sabar defines the Hebrew word for foreigner, *Gerim*, as being the equivalent to our "immigrants, foreigners, aliens, guest workers, shelter seekers, etc."[10] Two things pop out immediately. The first is that Leviticus 24:22 tells us, "You are to have the same law for the foreigner and the native-born. I am the Lord your God."[11] Please do not jump to the conclusion that the law in the verse is restricted to the legal codes that address our civic duties. Sabar goes on to say how those foreigners were, and in my view, are to be treated: "They have to be treated with justice and as equals to native citizens . . . reminding the Children of Israel that they, too, were once *gerim*, strangers in Egypt."[12] Treating outsiders as equals does not come naturally. It is an acquired skill that entails dedication and practice, as one does when learning a musical instrument or beginning a new hobby. But the book of Hebrews moves us on from treating the outsider fairly, to intentionally loving them, and then tells us what that love looks like.

Hebrews 13:1–3 reads, "Keep on loving one another as brothers and sisters. Do not forget to show hospitality to strangers, for by so doing some people have shown hospitality to angels without knowing it. Continue to remember those in prison as if you were together with them in prison, and those who are mistreated as if you yourselves were suffering."[13] Allow me to break this passage down a little. Treat the outsider as an insider, meaning like a family member who will always be family. Greet them with open arms because you never know who you are speaking with. A while back there was a story making the rounds about a CEO of a major department

9. Ps 146:6–10, NIV.
10. Sabar, "Gerim," para. 1.
11. Lev 24:22, NIV.
12. Sabar, "Gerim," para. 1.
13. Heb 13:1–3, NIV.

store chain who dressed like a homeless person, and then went to a few of the company's stores to see how he would be treated. It wasn't good! As a Black man I certainly can relate to that story. I would ask that you insert yourself and then try to relate to it as though it was happening to you.

SLAVERY AND SOCIOECONOMICS

Romans 1:20 reads, "For since the creation of the world God's invisible qualities—his eternal power and divine nature—have been clearly seen, being understood from what has been made."[14] Many people have used this text to prove that the natural world is but a reflection of God's intended will. It then follows that the hierarchies found in the animal kingdom reflect the intentions of God. That leaves many Christians who are comfortable living in a society that accepts racial hierarchies as the norm believing that the racially tiered economic system is also part of God's plan. That inevitably leads to some on top assuming that a God-ordained entitlement is the reason they are where they are. Notice how easy it was for Atlanta megachurch pastor Louis Giglio to conflate a politically structured racial hierarchy with the blessing of God. "We understand the curse that was slavery, white people do," Giglio said. "And we say that was bad, but we miss the blessing of slavery, that it actually built up the framework for the world that white people live in and lived in."[15]

RACIAL SOCIOECONOMICS

Once race is injected into any topic of conversation, even one such as economics which should be pretty straightforward, twisted logic is sure to follow. Prominent Christian author Tom Nelson acknowledges the criticism of the *blessing* of American chattel slavery in his book *The Economics of Neighborly Love*. He writes, "Critics point to dignity-defacing practices like slavery and colonization, suggesting these evils were the actual drivers of wealth creation."[16] Then he turns around and observes: "My sense is that a combination of spiritual, moral, cultural, political, legal, and technological factors has influenced the rapid trajectory of human betterment in the

14. Rom 1:20, NIV.
15. Burke, "Atlanta pastor," para. 3.
16. Nelson, *Economics*, 41.

last two hundred years."[17] That is a pretty long list of factors that are more responsible for America's wealth than running businesses with little or no overhead.

Nelson appears to be saying that the people who opposed slavery on both economic and moral grounds were off base. When people said slavery was a contributing factor to the ascendancy of the US to a world economic power they were simply wrong. Their view was it was actually mechanical advancements and the industrial revolution that lifted millions of white Americans out of poverty. There is undoubtedly some truth in that view. However, simple logic would suggest that if the slaves did not provide a great deal of economic benefit to white America, why have them? Historian Steven Mintz estimated, "Over the period of the Atlantic Slave Trade, from approximately 1526 to 1867, some 12.5 million slaves had been shipped from Africa, and 10.7 million had arrived in the Americas."[18] Again, if they were not needed, why go through all that trouble? Nelson, like many others today, seems to want a guilt-free story of the past treatment of African people on US soil. If I misinterpreted the author's intent I apologize. But it sure seems to me he looked at the brutally inhumane system that slavery was and understood it to be just a flaw in an otherwise great economic system.

Michael Sandel offered us an example of a frequent argument from those who deny both the brutality and the benefits that came with slavery in his book titled *Justice*, saying that the proof to either claim is sketchy. He wrote, "If it can be shown that those on the top are beneficiaries of past injustices—such as the enslavement of African-Americans and the expropriation of Native Americans—then, according to Nozick, a case could be made for remedying the injustice."[19] The problem with the "if it can be shown" proposition is that it is highly unlikely anyone involved in nefarious activities such as kidnapping people, followed by forced servitude, would write an accurate history of it. That is if they even realized what they were doing was nefarious to begin with. The harm this kind of narrative does is to lead millions of people to believe there really has never been much racism in America, ever! What follows might at least help us begin to question some of our present day assumptions about slavery that says it was simply an unfortunate sidenote in history.

17. Nelson, *Economics*, 42.

18. Mintz, "Historical Context," para. 1.

19. Sandel, *Justice*, 63.

FAIR TRADE LABOR

The Oxford Dictionary defines trade as "the action of buying and selling goods and services."[20] One unstated trade agreement between the enslaver and the enslaved was "we will trade you a lifestyle equal to ours in the future in exchange for your free labor now." That was the promise made to many enslaved Africans to get them to "behave better." Good behavior was defined by what was acceptable and profitable to the enslaver. Over time a theology was developed and taught to the enslaved people, that if they patiently endured their plight in this life, God would reward them in heaven. The slavers would have preachers speak of the splendor of heaven, and imply that if they were obedient and diligent in the jobs that God had provided for them, they would one day have a place in heaven. Peter Paris reports that some of the enslaved reached the logical conclusion that "I am having my hell now—when I die I will have my heaven ... Master is having his heaven now; when he dies he will have his hell."[21]

One old song makes reference to the fact that goods such as robes, i.e., clothing and shoes, were not distributed evenly. In fact, no one cared if the African did or did not have them. Africans who attended church on the weekend were expected to take comfort in Bible verses interpreted so as to keep slaves obsequious. One that was frequently preached to them read, "But seek first his kingdom and his righteousness, and all these things will be given to you as well."[22] Another favorite read, "And my God will meet all your needs according to the riches of his glory in Christ Jesus."[23] That would result in songs like the following sung on cotton fields all across the South as men, women, and children labored twelve hours a day under a hot sun.

> I got a robe, you got a robe
> All o' God's chillun got a robe
> When I get to heab'n I'm goin' to put on my robe
> I'm goin' to shout all ovah God's Heab'n
> Heab'n, Heab'n
> Ev'rybody talkin' 'bout heab'n ain't goin' dere
> Heab'n, Heab'n
> I'm goin' to shout all ovah God's Heab'n

20. Lexico.com, "Trade," line 1.

21. Paris, *Spirituality of African Peoples*, 64.

22. Matt 6:33, NIV.

23. Phil 4:19, NIV.

I got-a wings, you got-a wings
All o' God's chillun got-a wings
When I get to heab'n I'm goin' to put on my wings
I'm goin' to fly all ovah God's Heab'n
Heab'n, Heab'n
Ev'rybody talkin' 'bout heab'n ain't goin' dere
Heab'n, Heab'n
I'm goin' to fly all ovah God's Heab'n
I got shoes, you got shoes
All o' God's chillun got shoes
When I get to heab'n I'm goin' to put on my shoes
I'm goin' to walk all ovah God's Heab'n
Heab'n, Heab'n
Ev'rybody talkin' 'bout heab'n ain't goin' dere
Heab'n, Heab'n[24]

Peter Paris notes that "slaveholding Christianity did, in fact, posit segregated heaven."[25] Racism runs deep and the insidiousness of its hold on the psyche of people is evidenced in the attitudes of the white worshiping community. The idea that the kingdom of God was an extension of the earthly kingdom they had established resulted in a large number of Christians believing that there would be racial bodies in heaven. I point this out not for theological purposes, but as an example of twisted kingdom economics. That belief allowed people to be quite comfortable believing that separate was better in all areas of life right down to graveyards, and even God willed that segregation would be in force posthumously. What's next is flat-out bizarre.

STAY AWAY FROM ME

Jennifer Young wrote, "Until the 1950s, about 90 percent of all public cemeteries in the U.S. employed a variety of racial restrictions. Until recently, to enter a cemetery was to experience, as a University of Pennsylvania geography professor put it, the 'spatial segregation of the American dead.'"[26] Even when a religious cemetery was not entirely race restricted, different races were buried in separate parts of the cemetery, with whites usually getting the more attractive plots. The segregated cemeteries usually meant that

24. Pdinfo.com, "Public Domain Songs," para. 1.
25. Paris, *Spirituality of African Peoples*, 65.
26. Young, "Persistent Racism," para. 4.

groundskeepers kept the white areas immaculate while neglecting the Black areas.

For example, "In 2016, the city of Waco, Texas, issued an order to remove a fence in the city's public burial ground, Greenwood Cemetery . . . The cemetery had been racially segregated since it opened in the late 1800s. It was operated by two sets of caretakers, white and black, until the city took over the cemetery about 10 years ago."[27] Wow, it was believed that Black groundskeepers could in some way disturb a white person's eternal rest. It goes further. Consider another graveyard. "In the white Catholic section of the cemetery, there are flags on each of the veteran's tombstones honoring them for their services, whereas in the black section, there is nothing."[28] The article also points out that the white graves had headstones while the Black graves had rocks and sticks for markers. The fact that people who look like me could be hated after death brings tears to my eyes even while writing this. Think about it.

CHASING THE DREAM

I must share the takeaway I got from a book titled *The Upside-Down Kingdom*.[29] In the kingdom of God, of which economics are an important part, different rules apply. God spoke to Solomon and rewarded his upside-down and impractical view of economics. He had asked God to make him wise and not rich. That is not a trade many of us would make, right? In our culture if someone has money, people assume they are at least smart if not wise. That is why we often turn to wealthy entertainers, sports figures, and entrepreneurs for advice on many subjects on which they have absolutely no experience. Amazing right? With that in mind read what God told Solomon about his personal economics of being.

> "Since this is your heart's desire and you have not asked for wealth, possessions or honor, nor for the death of your enemies, and since you have not asked for a long life but for wisdom and knowledge to govern my people over whom I have made you king, therefore wisdom and knowledge will be given you. And I will also give you wealth, possessions and honor."[30]

27. Young, "Persistent Racism," para. 1.

28. Historyengine.richmond.edu, "Segregation Has Not Died," para. 3.

29. Kraybill, *The Upside-Down Kingdom*.

30. 2 Chr 1:11–12, NIV.

Let us contrast an ancient Greek king, Antiochus Epiphanes, who obviously did not see God's economic process as being practical. When he took power he had his picture stamped on the coinage along with the phrase, "King Antiochus God Manifest, Bearer of Victory."[31] He did this to poke at the religious Jews who found this offensive for several reasons. My reason for bringing this up is not the effect it had on them, but what his apparent intent might have been. Like now, money was an important commodity because it was used in daily transactions. Antiochus wanted people to see him, know of his power, and be thankful to him for their perceived well-being. There was no better way to accomplish that than to force them to see his likeness when they looked at their money. The king's overly inflated sense of self-worth and value made his place in history a little cloudy because "His eccentricities earned him the name Antiochus 'Epimanes' ('The Mad One'), a word play on his divine title 'Epiphanes.'"[32] His narcissistic behavior earned him another nickname in Jewish sources— "the wicked one." In a bit of irony the word *pig* is often associated with a greedy person. Antiochus ordered his soldiers "to force the Jews to sacrifice a pig to the Greek gods."[33] One would have to wonder what was in his heart to cause him to select that particular animal to be sacrificed by the Jewish people.

FAIR SHARE

I remember a candy bar routine that two comedians used to perform that cracked me up. It could also be a good illustration of the possible hazards that come with centralized distributive economics. The "brains" of the duo, the central planner, was given a candy bar. His sidekick asked for his share, at which time the brainiac broke it into two pieces. There was an immediate problem because the two pieces were not close to being equal in length. The brainiac gave his sidekick the much smaller piece, at which time the befuddled, frustrated, and not-so-smart one protested. In a very calm manner the brainiac explained each had one piece and so it was fair. Then the exasperated sidekick objected even more vociferously. Finally the brainiac gives in and indicates he will make the two shares equal. He then bites his larger piece at the point where it is about the size of his traveling partner's

31. Bibleodyssey.org, "Antiochus Epiphanes Coin."
32. Chosenpeople.com, "Antiochus iv," para. 1.
33. Chosenpeople.com, "Antiochus iv," para. 4.

portion and says, "There, now they are the same size, are you satisfied?" The brainiac had two options when the candy bar snapped in an uneven fashion. One, go get another candy bar insuring they would get the same amount. Two, convince his sidekick that his lesser amount is fair because it was now equal in size. Many argue that is what some economic systems do, convince the citizenry to do with less.

HOUSING MARKET CORRECTION

A market economy is based on the laws of supply and demand, private ownership, freedom of choice, and self-interest. People who believe a moral component exists within the framework of a market economy argue that when a deal between free beings is entered into everybody wins. I would ask you to consider whether or not two people entering into a deal are always on equal footing, or are their times when one side is "preying" on the other? If so, is that moral just because it is legal? Let me share one example where two parties did win, but in completely different ways.

Julaine and I knew a woman that had recently become a single mom with four teenaged kids. The ex-husband walked out for another woman and left her with a large mortgage that she was struggling to pay while working at a convenience store. Her home was up for sale but in ill repair and so there was not much interest. Additionally, it was just after the housing bubble burst in the US and home buyers were jittery. That is because no one wanted to offer 300k for a home that might be worth 250k in three months. At the exact same time there was a couple living out of state that was looking to move into the single mom's area. The couple had their home up for sale in their home state but there were few interested buyers for the same reasons. Somehow they found each other and the couple bought the home. The single mom was able to rent from the new owners until their home in the other state sold. On the surface it seemed like a win/win. However, a problem did arise after the couple moved, plumbing issues and a few other things that were not disclosed. The new owners had to put several thousand dollars into the home just to be able to move in.

Did they both win? I am sure the single mom's family breathed a sigh of relief when their daughter was able to separate herself from her burdensome mortgage. And the other couple was able to move to the new area without having to fly out and look for housing, never knowing when that would end in a purchase. The reality is that both parties "got something" out of the deal. But in a strictly economic sense, it is probably true that the buyer took a bigger financial hit than the seller. Yet at the end of the day both parties were happy. Do you think that outcome is typical or unusual? Speaking of housing, allow me to share some housing market incorrectness from my early years.

BILL AND XANTHYNE

Consider some funky ways that whites outside of the South once treated Blacks. There are many people that have convinced themselves that racism was restricted to the South and that Northerners were above that type of behavior. If that is you, I hope what follows will be an eye-opener. Richard Rothstein wrote an excellent book titled *The Color of Law*, but it is the subtitle, "A Forgotten History of How Government Segregated America," that I want to draw your attention to. My reason for sharing this with you is twofold. The first is that this book contains many largely ignored facts about our country's racial history. The second is that one of the stories highlighted in this book is actually my story.

My parents, Bill and Xanthyne Calhoun, were born and raised in the tightly segregated states of Arkansas and Texas. Like most parents they desired a better life for their children, which ended with them leaving the South and migrating to what they thought would be a better all-around situation in California. It was the desire of a better life that ended with themselves, along with their two young children, living for a time in Richmond, California. Our house was not the fine house that pop singers Crosby, Stills, Nash & Young sang about because the "federally financed housing for African-Americans in Richmond was poorly constructed,"[34] and "it was officially and explicitly segregated."[35]

> The Richmond Police as well as the housing authority pressed the city recreation department to forbid integrated activities, so where projects for whites and projects for blacks shared recreational and sports facilities, the authority designated special hours for African-American use. The authority maintained social programs for whites and blacks—Boy and Girl Scout troops and movie screenings for example. A policy of segregation was adopted, explained by the authority's director, for the purpose of keeping

34. Rothstein, *Color of Law*, 5.
35. Rothstein, *Color of Law*, 5.

"social harmony" . . . Another housing authority official insisted that, "Negroes from the south would rather be by themselves."[36]

My parents left their relatives and all they knew hoping that my brother and I would not face the same racial treatment they had endured, only to find a subtle and surreptitious version of it outside the South. Ira Berlin noted that during the time that my family was settling in California, "The level of racial segregation, the indices of dissimilarity—which measured the degree of segregation—reached 90 percent,"[37] not just in Richmond but nationally. The story many people told themselves to justify the exclusion of people like my family was simply not true. "Negroes" did not want to be by themselves, they were forced to be by themselves. And consider this example of a financial repercussion that kind of racism produces in an area where I have lived: "Homeowners' median net worth is 80 times renters' median net worth, according to a 2019 Census Bureau study. That same study found that whites had a median household wealth of $139,300, compared with $12,780 for black households."[38] I hope you can see that excluding not only affects where Black people live, it also affects how they live. Sure, everyone will face challenges in life. However, it should not be overlooked that minority groups face those typical challenges *plus* the ones placed on them as a result of who they are.

THE FUNK OF IT

Shortly after I moved to Los Angeles from the Bay Area of northern California where Richmond is located, I met a white family named Koppel. I met the oldest brother first and he became one of my closer friends. In time I became close to the entire family. In fact we became so close that I called them my LA family. The family owned a small business and several of our mutual friends worked for them in various capacities. One year Rare Earth dissolved and I was out of work. My daughter had just been born and I was a wreck financially. One day I decided to share my situation with the younger Koppel brother, who was now running the family business. We talked for awhile and then he turned to me and said, "Cal, you know we are always in need of good sales reps to encourage our customers to buy some

36. Rothstein, *Color of Law,* 5.

37. Berlin, *Making of African America,* 190.

38. Lerner, "Black Home Ownership," para. 32.

of our other products. You are bright, articulate, personable and you would make a great salesman for our company. But here is the problem, I know our customers and they would never order anything from you." So, I wound up working with the older brother part time in a job that did not involve customer contact and paid significantly less.

Please do not write off my experience as an anomaly or an isolated case. I think you can understand that if one people group has purposefully distanced themselves from another, it is highly unlikely they would turn right around and do business with them in any significant way. Taking this into consideration, you might want to rethink the impression you get seeing a young Black male struggling at the lower rung of the employment spectrum. He may not be there for the reasons you assume, such as lack of initiative, education, or skill. There might be more employers out there reaching the same conclusion my friend did than you would like to believe. Remember, there are many perceptual streams, as Clifford Coulter so passionately sang, that can decide what kind of shape a person is going to be in. One of those streams may be an unconscious desire to maintain social superiority. And there is probably no better way to achieve that than through the control of economic opportunity. That is the Funk of it!

10

THE HEART OF BEING

Social theorist Christian Smith opened his excellent book *Moral Believ-ing Animals* with this question: "What kind of animals are human be-ings . . . How can we describe their peculiar characteristics?"[1] I put it to you, what kind of animals are we? And secondarily, what kind of person are you? Roger Scruton noted that "the term person comes from the Latin persona,"[2] adding that persona originally referred to the way actors hid behind masks to obscure their true personalities. He noted that the philosopher Boethius defined a person as "an individual substance of a rational nature . . . and therefore could not cease to be a person without ceasing to be."[3]

The word *be* is the key to the fullest understanding of what I am at-tempting to convey in this final chapter. We have all heard people use a version of, "Well, I am human after all," in order to make an excuse for some perceived failure. What did they mean? *Merriam-Webster* says when the word *human* is used as a noun, it means a "bi-ped primate mammal,"[4] an animal. The word *be-ing* has to do with the way a human exists. That is true whether the word *human* is used as an adjective or a noun, and that gets us to the heart of the matter. What I write in this chapter is predicated on the belief that we have been created as imaginative, self-reflective, be-ings that are human.

1. Smith, *Moral Believing Animals*, 3.
2. Scruton, *Soul of the World*, 29.
3. Scruton, *Soul of the World*, 29.
4. *Merriam-Webster*, "Human," line 1.

When speaking of "the all-singing, all-dancing human being,"[5] physiologist Denis Noble drew an analogy between our physiological makeup, meaning our cells and organs, and a musical orchestra that is made up of different instrumentalists working together to perform music. He went on to elaborate on the cellular components of a human being, such as the heart muscle, lungs, brain, and even our endocrine glands. Then he pointed out that our "heart muscle cells work somewhat differently than our skeletal muscle cells, but the two also have a lot in common."[6] Then he notes, significantly: "It absolutely is not possible to understand the working of the heart as an organ at a purely molecular level."[7] I would say one reason for that can be found in Scriptures that attest to "the unique status of the heart as representative of the essential self."[8] Yes, the physical heart pumps life-enabling oxygenated blood to the body. But it is the biblical heart that pumps life-giving spiritually infused nutrients to the soul. I ask that you hold on to the following two Scriptures as you read ahead: "In their hearts humans plan their course,"[9] and "Guard your heart, for everything you do flows from it."[10]

These Scriptures reveal different operations of the biblical heart. The first passage speaks to the source of our being, while the second energizes it. The first is concerned with the root of the decision-making process. The second identifies the particular actions produced by those decisions. According to Paul Pearsall, "Unlike the brain the heart knows it cannot be 'the mind' but that together with the brain and body it forms a Mind of which it is a key part."[11] James Peters voiced a similar understanding when he wrote, "One cannot function rationally in isolation from the heart."[12] To simplify just a little, we are who we are as a result of what the heart contributes to our being. We will soon see that there are scientists who believe we should omit the word *heart* from any discussion about what makes us who we are.

5. Noble, *Music of Life*, 82.

6. Noble, *Music of Life*, 83.

7. Noble, *Music of Life*, 84.

8. David, *Jurisprudence and Theology*, 106.

9. Prov 16:9, NIV.

10. Prov 4:23, NIV.

11. Pearsall, *Heart's Code*, 207.

12. Peters, *Logic of the Heart*, 18.

THE BEING HEART

That said, let us change lanes and discuss the heart of being conceptually by looking at it in a purely existential context. Let us try to "stand outside of ourselves" for a moment in order to examine the way we relate to Jesus. This can be seen in the contrast between Paul's idea of what it means to believe in Christ as a matter of faith and *being* in Christ, which in many ways is philosophical. Believing in Christ is concerned with learning and accepting certain facts about him. Being in Christ is a total commitment to the reality that as a Christian your life has a new address. And that address is not located in cities such as Austin, Lagos, or Mexico City, but in the kingdom of God. The Orthodox Saint Gregory highlighted the difference between believing and being this way: "True opinion is not the knowledge discovered through words and reasoning, but that which is demonstrated through both deeds and life."[13]

The way I am applying St. Gregory's words can be seen in the following illustration. If a police officer were to inquire who I was, the expectation would be that I know my name, address, and date of birth. Once those facts became known to her the officer would be satisfied. However, if this follow-up question had been asked by the officer, "where are you spiritually," my answer would have been harder to nail down. That is because the kingdom Jesus spoke of is not a temporal or material place that can be pointed to like a street address. Our spiritual addresses are impossible to plot on any type of map. That is why the heart of being is best understood in a way that is similar to the words of Graeme Nicholson, "Being is a possibility . . . an openness to the future that is never closed up, never finished, a perpetual becoming."[14] The Bible says that a prophet named Ezra "prepared his heart"[15] for God. I can think of no better way to a prepare a heart for what life may bring than to have a heart completely open to the will of God.

BLURRED VISION

Earlier I put forward my belief that there are many people, even some Christians, who see religion as being inadequate to solve complex problems such as racial division. That view is understandable when people of no

13. Tanev and Bradshaw, *Energy in Orthodox Theology*, 150.
14. Nicholson, *Justifying Our Existence*, 22.
15. Ezra 7:10, KJV.

faith observe the way some of the more popular expressions of Christianity operate. When the church has its eyes on what it is that is changing more than timeless truths, it makes it difficult for the observer to see what it stands for. What they see is some branches of the church responding to the ever-changing cultural trends, while other churches only appear to be responsive to the felt needs of their attenders. That results in the uninitiated seeing the church as an organization that is, to quote cultural icon Bob Dylan, "blowing in the wind."

Another reason for non-Christians discounting the value of faith is that religion is often characterized as being history's greatest divider. A common critique I hear is that we should remember all of the wars that have been fought in the name of religion. That view is an unfair and inaccurate assessment. Writing on race has taught me that people can and do find many ways to dislike others. And they do it for the most benign and inane reasons, such as skin color, country of origin, or being a Dodger fan rather than a Giants fan. Put in the simplest terms, when you want to justify your dislike for those dreaded other folks, "any ole excuse will do."

Let us break down the "war" excuse just a little and try on this analogy to see if it fits. Suppose that you woke up one morning and read a headline that said a fight had broken out at a local sports bar between fans of two opposing pro football teams. Would you say, "Sports are no good, look at all the fights they have caused"? No, you would probably read the rest of the article to see who the drunken immature men were that behaved badly. Maybe you would even be curious about whether or not they were hurt or arrested. However, you would not hold the pro franchises accountable for the actions of their fans. And you would probably not vow to never set foot in a pro football stadium again—or even a bar or airport that has a game on its television. Yet we have no problem linking age-old political disputes with religion. People gladly shift the blame from politicians to religion's visible expression called the church. Even when it is clear that it was the armies of some form of a sovereign state that invaded another country or were involved in genocide. Maybe people should not let the fact that human beings attend church, and live in a nation-state, blur the line between the two so much that they are not able to tell them apart.

CLOGGED SPIRITUAL ARTERIES

I have a young friend who jokingly refers to me as a "religious hippie." That is actually appropriate because a hippie and a religious person may have been more similar than different in their approach to life. Moreover, it may be an attitude worth revisiting. A description of a hippie found on the Britannica web page says, "The Hippies advocated nonviolence and love . . . They promoted openness and tolerance as alternatives."[16] I would argue with anyone that the values just listed make a compelling vision for what it means to be a loving human being.

Love and peace, coupled with an openness to love the other, should be two of the primary foci of the church. And they should also be something the attenders attempt to live out daily. Unfortunately, being connected to the other by Jesus' love is not all that high on most Christians' priority list. And this love for enemies stuff? Forget it. However, let us consider what the early Christians held dear to their hearts. "Much of what Jesus taught seems to have been followed closely during the first several hundred years after his death and resurrection . . . Values like nonparticipation in war, simple living, inclusivity, and love of enemies."[17] Then at some point in time it appears the cares of life began to block the love that had flowed out of the hearts of the early Christians. A form of paralysis set in that immobilized the church and kept it from its mission of inclusivity and connectedness.

Just think, the early Christians were intentional about connecting with and loving their enemies. So much so that it was evident to those outside the faith writing the histories. We sure are not there today, are we? Rather than feeling a connection with people that we disagree with, we feel quite comfortable feeling a deep seated antipathy towards them. Think Republican if you are a Democrat, and think Democrat if you are Republican. What has caused narrowly targeted love to be the outcome of Jesus' message?

Perhaps we can look at some of the diseases that cause paralysis in other areas of our lives for a clue. I have suffered from high cholesterol and my doctor is always on me to lower it. Her concern is that if I leave it unchecked it could lead to a stroke, which is the leading cause of paralysis in the US. This is how high cholesterol can lead to a stoke: "Carotid artery disease occurs when fatty deposits clog the blood vessels that deliver blood

16. Britannica.com, "Hippie," para 3.
17. Rohr, "Early Christian Values," para. 1.

to your brain and head . . . The blockage increases your risk of stroke."[18] There is another site that gives us some additional information about that process. "The carotid arteries branch off from the aorta . . . a short distance from the heart, and extend upward through the neck carrying oxygen-rich blood to the brain."[19] So this added information includes the fact that one reason for a stroke is the blockage occurs close to the heart. Maybe the same could be said if we suffer from spiritual artery disease. We allow our careers, our politics, and our busy lifestyles to create blockages between our brains and what should be close to our biblical hearts. It is crystal clear throughout the Bible that the heart can be hardened. Not only Pharaoh's heart, but the people of God are equally susceptible, as Paul reminded us in Acts saying, "This people's heart has become calloused; they hardly hear with their ears, and they have closed their eyes."[20] God does have a plan for your spiritual heart and that plan is for it to be transformed into one that is similar to his. Let us look at some of the impediments to that being a reality.

NATURE'S CHAINS

The neuroscientist and philosopher Sam Harris opens his *Free Will* with an argument that says that free will is an illusion and nothing more. He goes on to say that popular conceptions of this illusion "seem to rest on two assumptions: (1) Each of us could have behaved differently than we did in the past, and (2) That we are the conscious source of most of our thoughts in the present."[21] Then he embarks on a swift journey through his short book to prove that you lack the free will to put it down. (Sorry, I couldn't help myself.) That is because later in the chapter he writes that, "Some moments before you decide what you are going to do next—a time in which you subjectively appear to have the complete freedom to behave however you please—your brain has already determined what you will do."[22] So the heart of our being resides in a "neuropsychological self" that waits for marching orders from our subconscious brain?

The basis for my pushback against his theory is not philosophical, even theological, it is funknological. If I am understanding his premise

18. Mayoclinic.org, "Carotid Artery," para.1.
19. Columbianeurology.org, "Carotid Artery," para. 2.
20. Acts 28:27, NIV.
21. Harris, *Free Will*, 6.
22. Harris, *Free Will*, 9.

correctly, my bass playing is not the result of a creative mind instructing my fingers which way to manipulate the strings on my guitar. When I think that it is me playing the Funk, it is actually the result of a physical organ I possess called the brain telling my fingers to play F, then G, then A, in time with the drummer. The music comes out of me without my knowledge, or permission for that matter. I am not a scientist, but if I carry his thesis to its logical end, then it is my body reacting to the natural laws of nature that creates the music I play. If that is the case, then why haven't those same natural laws produced a pit bull that sings like Rihanna or Aretha Franklin? I use that somewhat ridiculous analogy to point out that natural causes may not be the best answer for all that happens in the world. Let us stretch this funky example a little further.

Let me say up front that I wholeheartedly believe scientific theories are beneficial because they initiate investigation and that in turn leads to progress. But there are times when it might be wise to step back, put some simple flesh and blood on them, then scrutinize what it is we accept a little more thoroughly. For example, if Swiss bodies produce polka music because that people group inhabits the Alps, then maybe the reason Black bodies produce blues music is because they inhabit the rural South. But what happens if those same Black bodies migrate to the North? Do they magically acquire the ability to play Funk? That's not the way it works. I can create a pretty funky bass line at the drop of a hat because I possess the DNA of a really creative person named God. God freely created and made Jimi in his image. Being an image bearer means I am free to create too. And there are no chains, natural or otherwise, preventing me from doing so. That may not be scientific but it is scriptural.

Harris suggests that the reason we delude ourselves into believing we have free will is because we don't understand the way natural cause-and-effect relationships control everything. I would wonder at this point how Harris can be sure of what he posited if he is not the person making choices about what to include and exclude. Does he really believe that it is his neurological system responding to unidentified stimuli making them for him? Said another way, how does he know he can trust his brain if it is just an organ functioning in much the same way his kidney or liver does—that is, operating on its own volition? If that were true, why hold anyone accountable for behaviors that originate beyond their control, like starting wars or committing crimes? Actually, Harris does offer some compelling scientific theories to buttress his arguments. But this section is about who we are and not what we do, and so you will have to get your hands on some of his books to see what those are. Let us turn now to a faith-based response to what was just put forward by Harris.

UNCHAIN MY HEART

In a moment we will see that the Bible does not accept what I believe to be Harris's errant deterministic view of human will and neither do the courts. Harris says, "The intention to do one thing and not another does not originate in consciousness."[23] Allow me to put some flesh and blood on what I believe to be a theory based on abstractions. Let us imagine that I am standing before a judge being charged with assault. The judge decides to get my side of the story and asks me what happened. I respond, "Well, your honor, I was at a gathering of friends when my liver began reacting to the beer I was drinking, and my kidney began reacting to the sugar in the cake. All of a sudden my fists reacted to an insult that my ears heard, and it appears I clobbered the guy who said it." Perhaps once the judge was able to control the inadvertent snicker my answer had produced, she might ask me to explain what I was saying.

Grateful for the opportunity to have a redo, I decide to give it a go, only this time I would utilize Harris's physicalist view to its fullest. Dr. Michael Graziano sheds light ahead of my new application of this view, writing, "One of the underlying assumptions of brain science is that information is computed by neurons."[24] Now using my limited grasp of neuroscience, I explain to the judge that the liver neuron stopped me from drinking too much. Then the kidney neuron fired off orders to put the cake down. But for some reason unknown to me, the hand neuron allowed my fist to wind up on the person's jaw before the ear neuron could accept his apology. Please do not interpret what I have just said as some type of sarcastic meaningless diatribe directed toward the writings of Sam Harris and physicalism. It is not. As Richard Swinburne noted, "There just are what I describe as 'physical events,' and 'pure mental events' (including conscious events) which are different from each other and philosophers should face up to this."[25]

23. Harris, *Free Will*, 8.
24. Graziano, *God, Soul, Mind, Brain*, 92.
25. Swinburne, *Mind*, 98.

FREE TO CHOOSE

Let us look at two biblical examples to help us get our hearts in the right place. Joshua shouted to a recalcitrant Israel, "Choose for yourselves this day whom you will serve."[26] Moses told the Israelites to "choose life, that you and your offspring may live."[27] I ask you to choose this day whom you will love. The point being, there really is a choice! It is not possible that Moses and Joshua were both unaware that their target audiences lacked the ability to choose, which would make their words a waste of time. Is it possible that some have convinced themselves that they do not have the ability to choose? Apparently Moses was really confused because he said that what "I command you today is not too hard for you."[28] So does this mean the Bible not only teaches that it is possible to make choices, it also teaches that at times they are easy to do? Yes! The BBC web page dedicated to religious studies reported, "Most Jews believe that when God created them, he gave them free will. This is the idea that people are able to make their own decisions and distinguish right from wrong."[29]

The former Chief Rabbi of Great Britain, Jonathan Sacks, suggested that the proof of our having free will could be found in teshuvah, which is the process of repentance. The way I understand repentance in Judaism is that it entails more than remorse for bad behavior. Doing teshuvah requires that a person admit to their bad behavior and then do something to make restitution for any damage caused by it. Following that, they take whatever steps necessary to restore the relationship to its previous condition. All three of those elements require purposeful action, meaning a person chooses to do it. Rabbi Sacks offered an example to illustrate what that looks like. A person sins. Then an opportunity presents itself to engage in the same behavior in an identical circumstance. But this time the person chooses not to engage in that same behavior. The fact that the person acted differently in an exact same circumstance would be conclusive proof that human beings are in fact "free to choose."

26. Josh 24:15, NIV.
27. Deut 30:19, NIV.
28. Deut 30:11, NIV.
29. Bbc.co.uk, "Covenant," para. 2.

FREE TO LIVE

The Oxford Dictionary defines an emotion as "a natural instinctive state of mind deriving from one's circumstances, mood, or relationships with others."[30] It is the "with others" that I want to focus on. Roger Scruton wrote, "Until realized in the objective world, freedom is a dream."[31] Then he goes on to say that a dream can become a nightmare because, "he [a subject], exercising his freedom in a world of objects, enters into conflict with others who are doing the same."[32] That is a problem, isn't it? I had a neighbor in Boca Raton who encircled his entire yard with bushes that grew over seven feet tall. Good for him. The thing is before he did that, I had an unobstructed view of a golf course. His choice ended that, and so too bad for me. That leads to the question of how do we give others freedom to live, if that freedom inevitably leads to limiting it for someone else? That conundrum exposes the holes in the idea that freedom is synonymous with unfettered individual rights. Freedom can be misused and abused.

Racism is an abuse of human freedom because the powerful group uses its freedom to intentionally trample on the rights of the weaker group, thereby limiting theirs. Once in motion, the only chance of curtailing the expansion of that abuse is for the powerful to willingly undergo a change of perception. That willingness should emanate from somewhere deep down in a person's heart if it is to be there for the long haul. David prayed for a heart that is pure; not a different heart, or even a sin-free, or a perfect heart—but one that could function in a new way. One that would be open to embracing the totality of the will of God even when that plan might be mysterious and challenging. It needs to be said that any activity that will curtail the spread of racism will most likely involve some challenge and mystery. Søren Kierkegaard suggested in *Fear and Trembling* the existence of something he called a "paradoxical movement of faith."

The paradox emerged from Abraham's willingness to sacrifice something he loved and mustering the personal faith required to actually do it. Part of the faith that Kierkegaard addresses is that Abraham must have had to overcome a tremendous amount of anxiety at the thought of killing his son *before* he journeyed to Moriah. If you are white, I am encouraging you to free yourself of any anxiety you might have at the prospect of entering

---

30. Lexico.com, "Emotion."

31. Scruton, *Soul of the World*, 111.

32. Scruton, *Soul of the World*, 111.—

into intimate relationships with a people group that you have typically avoided. That can be done the same way that Abraham pushed through his anxieties, through dependence on an overcoming faith.

FREE TO GIVE

If you are wondering why this book will end with the topic of giving, the answer is simple but not obvious. Much of our teaching time on Sunday mornings is spent informing people what it is God wants to do in their lives. A few years ago I was driving to a pastors conference with a colleague and he asked what I thought God was doing in my life. For some reason I responded by saying something that was probably inappropriate. I said that I was more concerned about what I was doing in God's life than what he was doing in mine. Looking back at that awkward moment I can see that my answer does expose an oversight in the way we do faith. It is also a reason why this book ends with giving. In fact, giving may actually be at the heart of the Christian message. It certainly is the ultimate end of the heart of being. Paul reminded us of something Jesus said about giving in Acts 20:35, "In everything I did, I showed you that by this kind of hard work we must help the weak, remembering the words the Lord Jesus himself said: 'It is more blessed to give than to receive.'"

Now consider this sequence of events that illustrates the divine heart of being. God gave his son, Jesus gave his life, and the Spirit gave and gives us life. The question that leaves us with is what would you be willing to give in order to usher in, let's say, the political and economic systems just discussed? Would you be willing to give your all against racism *and* for racial justice? Aligning yourself with those who have been affected by racism in order to pursue justice for them will cost you something if you are white. The key words here are *aligning with*, rather than *doing something for*. Few are willing to pay the toll to cross the bridge into Black or any other marginalized group's environment and challenge the dispensers of injustice. To ignore injustice is to deny that God loves those you have shut your heart's door to just as much as he loves you. Yes, loving those who have been marginalized by social status, race, and an economic system designed to exclude them is an affair of the heart. The transformed heart spoken of earlier is not a reference to a new and improved version of the pre-transformed heart, it is a visible version of the heart of Jesus.

THE FUNK OF IT

The Funk music that we opened this book with existed because the Father of Funk, James Brown, found an unlimited number of ways to create Funk music on the first beat of the measure, or "the one." In the Bible it is written that when a marriage happens two people become one flesh and there are many Christians that accept that as being possible. When a person is baptized into the Christian faith it is done in the name of the Father, Son, and Holy Spirit, which is Trinitarian theology. Most Christians accept that three persons can exist as one unified entity called God. The majority of Christians living in the United States will affirm the part of the Pledge of Allegiance that says "one nation, indivisible" when it is referring to fifty states comprising the United States of America.

Yet when Jimi Calhoun says that it is possible for the human species to live together "on the one," meaning as one race, somehow that idea is taken to be unnatural, impossible, unrealistic, and definitely impractical. Then I am painted as an idealistic utopian dreamer, or a religious hippie. Why? Just in case you are wondering, I plead guilty to every one of those charges. As we close this out, please consider this one last illustration. If one can accept two becoming one in marriage, where each partner seeks the well-being of the other . . . If one can accept three persons functioning as one God where each one seeks the well-being of the other . . . And if one can accept fifty independent states being one country with each state seeking the well-being of the other . . . it should follow that four, five, six, or even seven "different races" that make up one humanity can seek the well-being of the other. That is the Funk of it on the one!

BIBLIOGRAPHY

Abc7.com. "George Floyd: Former Minneapolis officer Derek Chauvin released on bond in George Floyd case." https://abc7.com/derek-chauvin-jail-release-george-floyd-officer-who-knelt-on-minneapolis-charges/6843265/.

Ackroyd, Peter. *Tudors.* New York: Thomas Dunne, 2012.

Allen, Zita. "Free to Dance: Behind The Dance." https://www.thirteen.org/freetodance/behind/behind_slaveships.html.

Amazon.com. *The Black Russian.* https://smile.amazon.com/dp/B009W74JZY/ref=rdr_kindle_ext_tmb.

Andrews, Dale P. *Practical Theology for Black Churches.* Louisville: Westminster John Knox, 2002.

Archives.gov. "FDR's First Inaugural Address Declaring 'War' on the Great Depression." https://www.archives.gov/education/lessons/fdr-inaugural.

Augustine. *Saint Augustine's Confessions.* Translated by Henry Chadwick. Oxford: Oxford University Press, 1991.

Baker, Bruce E. "Buck Dancing." https://www.ncpedia.org/buck-dancing.

Bates, Stephen. "The Hidden Holocaust." https://www.theguardian.com/theguardian/1999/may/13/features11.g22.

Bbc.com. "Breonna Taylor: What happened on the night of her death?" https://www.bbc.com/news/world-us-canada-54210448.

Bbc.co.uk. "Covenant and Mitzvot." https://www.bbc.co.uk/bitesize/guides/zfwr97h/revision/1.

Bell, Derrick. *Gospel Choirs.* New York: Basic, 1996.

Berkovits, Eliezer. *God, Man, and History.* Jerusalem: Shalom, 2014.

Berlin, Ira. *The Making of African America.* New York: Penguin, 2010.

Bibleodyssey.org. "Antiochus Epiphanes Coin." http://www.bibleodyssey.org/en/tools/image-gallery/a/antiochus-iv-epiphanes-coin.

Biderman, Chris. "Transcript: Colin Kaepernick addresses sitting during national anthem." https://ninerswire.usatoday.com/2016/08/28/transcript-colin-kaepernick-addresses-sitting-during-national-anthem/.

Blumberg, Naomi. "Vile or Visionary?: 11 Art Controversies of the Last Four Centuries." https://www.britannica.com/list/vile-or-visionary-11-art-controversies-of-the-last-four-centuries.

Boahen, A. Adu. *African Perspectives on European Colonialism.* New York: African Diasporic, 1987.

Bolden, Tony. *The Funk Era and Beyond.* New York: Palgrave MacMillan, 2008.

Brainyquote.com. "Aristotle." https://www.brainyquote.com/quotes/aristotle_148501.

———. "Mark Twain." https://www.brainyquote.com/quotes/mark_twain_121081.

Britannica.com. "Aboriginal Peoples in Australian Society: Early alien contact." https://www.britannica.com/topic/Australian-Aboriginal/Aboriginal-peoples-in-Australian-society#ref256946.

———. "Hippie." https://www.britannica.com/topic/hippie%20para%203.

———. "New York slave rebellion." https://www.britannica.com/event/New-York-slave-rebellion-of-1712.

———. "Sierra Leone." https://www.britannica.com/place/Sierra-Leone/Sports-and-recreation#ref541017.

———. "Thespis." https://www.britannica.com/biography/Thespis-Greek-poet.

Brodkin, Karen. *How Jews Became White Folks & What That Says About Race in America*. New Brunswick, NJ: Rutgers University Press, 2004.

Brown, Frank Burch. *Religious Aesthetics*. Princeton, NJ: Princeton University Press, 1989.

Buber, Martin. *I and Thou*. New York: Charles Scribner's Sons, 1958.

Burke, Minyvonne. "Atlanta pastor who suggested slavery was a 'blessing' to white people apologizes." https://www.nbcnews.com/news/us-news/atlanta-pastor-who-suggested-slavery-was-blessing-white-people-apologizes-n1231325.

Burke, Siobhan. "Dancing Bodies That Proclaim: Black Lives Matter." https://www.nytimes.com/2020/06/09/arts/dance/dancing-protests-george-floyd.html.

Burton, Nylah. "Black Jews Are Being Chased Out Of the Jewish Community By Racism. Here Are Their Stories." https://forward.com/opinion/408769/black-jews-are-being-chased-out-of-the-jewish-community-by-racism-here-are/.

Calhoun, Jimi. *The Art of God*. Eugene, OR: Cascade, 2015.

———. *A Story of Rhythm and Grace*. Eugene, OR: Cascade, 2018.

Carrega, Christina, and Sabina Ghebremedhi. "Inside the Investigation of Breonna Taylor's Killing." https://abcnews.go.com/US/timeline-inside-investigation-breonna-taylors-killing-aftermath/story?id=71217247.

Cdc.gov. "Attitudinal." https://www.cdc.gov/ncbddd/disabilityandhealth/disability-barriers.html#.

Chosenpeople.com. "Antiochus iv from Divine to Madman." https://www.chosenpeople.com/site/antiochus-iv-from-divine-to-madman.

Chuck, Elizabeth. "Michael Slager Testifies About Killing Walter Scott: It's Been a Nightmare." https://www.nbcnews.com/storyline/walter-scott-shooting/michael-slager-testifies-about-killing-walter-scott-it-s-been-n689691.

Citymayors.com. "Europe's Largest Cities." http://www.citymayors.com/features/euro_cities1.html.

Clinton, George, and Ben Greenman. *Brothas Be, Yo Like George*. New York: Atria, 2014.

Colorado.edu. "Illusion and Reality: The Science of Perception." https://www.colorado.edu/cuwizards/illusion-and-reality-science-perception.

Columbianeurology.org. "Carotid Artery Disease." https://www.columbianeurology.org/neurology/staywell/carotid-artery-disease.

Cook, Faith. *Zachary Macaulay*. Darlington, UK: EP, 2012.

Cottingham, John. *In Search of the Soul*. Princeton, NJ: Princeton University Press, 2020.

Crf-usa.org. "A Brief History of Jim Crow." https://www.crf-usa.org/black-history-month/a-brief-history-of-jim-crow.

David, Joseph E. *Jurisprudence and Theology: In Late Ancient and Medieval Jewish Thought*. New York: Springer, 2014.

Daynes, Sarah, and Orville Lee. *Desire for Race*. Cambridge: Cambridge University Press, 2008.

De Botton, Alain. *Status Anxiety*. New York: Vintage, 2005.

De Botton, Alain, and John Armstrong. *Art as Therapy*. New York: Phaidon, 2016.

Delgado, Richard, et al. *Critical Race Theory*. New York: NYU Press, 2017.

Dictionary.cambridge.net. "Curriculum Vitae." https://dictionary.cambridge.org/us/dictionary/english/curriculum-vitae.

———. "Signification." https://dictionary.cambridge.org/us/dictionary/english/signification.

———. "Fragility." https://dictionary.cambridge.org/us/dictionary/english/fragility.

———. "Funk." https://dictionary.cambridge.org/us/dictionary/english/funk.

Dosick, Wayne D. *Living Judaism*. San Francisco: HarperOne, 2010.

Doumbia, Adama, and Naomi Doumbia. *The Way of The Elders*. Saint Paul, MN: Llewellyn, 2004.

Dryness, Richard. *A Poetic Theology: God and the Poetics of Everyday Life*. Grand Rapids: Eerdmans, 2011.

Eagleton, Terry. *The Idea of Culture*. Oxford: Basil Blackwell, 2000.

———. *Ideology of The Aesthetic*. Oxford: Basil Blackwell, 1990.

Ellul, Jaques. *The Presence of the Kingdom*. Colorado Springs, CO: Helmers & Howard, 1989.

Espn.com. "Roger Goodell: 'Wish we had listened earlier' to what Colin Kaepernick was protesting." https://www.espn.com/nfl/story/_/id/29727180/wished-listened-earlier-colin-kaepernick-was-protesting.

Faber, Roland, and Jeremy Fackenthal. *Theopoetic Folds*. New York: Fordham University Press, 2013.

Figes, Orlando. "Russia and Europe." https://www.bbvaopenmind.com/en/articles/russia-and-europe/.

Fox, John. *Poetic Medicine*. New York: Tarcher Putnam, 1997.

Fuer, Alan. "Black New Yorkers Are Twice as Likely to Be Stopped by the Police, Data Shows." https://www.nytimes.com/2020/09/23/nyregion/nypd-arrests-race.html.

Funkmysoul.gr. "Leon's Creation." https://www.funkmysoul.gr/leons-creation-1970-this-is-the-beginning/.

Gadamer, Hans-Georg. *Truth and Method*. London: Bloomsbury Academic, 2013.

Gallup. "Research Finds Fragile Community." https://www.prnewswire.com/news-releases/cao-gallup-research-finds-fragile-community-residents-struggling-in-key-aspects-of-their-lives-as-pandemic-unrest-hit-301107195.html.

Gates, Louis Henry, Jr. *The Signifying Monkey: A Theory of African American Literary Criticism*. Oxford: Oxford University Press, 1988.

George, Alice. "The 1968 Kerner Commission Got It Right, But Nobody Listened." https://www.smithsonianmag.com/smithsonian-institution/1968-kerner-commission-got-it-right-nobody-listened-180968318/.

George, Nelson, and Alan Leeds, eds. *The James Brown Reader*. New York: Plume, 2008.

Glassner, Barry. *The Culture of Fear*. New York: Basic, 1999.

Goodreads.com. "Humankind." https://www.goodreads.com/quotes/13681-humankind-cannot-bear-very-much-reality.

———. "Jane Austen." https://www.goodreads.com/quotes/195631-do-you-dance-mr-darcy-darcy-not-if-i-can.

Google.com. "Rebellion." https://www.google.com/search?client=safari&rls=en&q=rebellion&ie=UTF-8&oe=UTF-8.

Gossett, Thomas F. *Race: The History of an Idea in America.* New York: Schocken, 1965.

Gottwald, Norman K. *Social Justice and the Hebrew Bible.* Eugene, OR: Cascade, 2016.

Goymer, P. "Bird Behaviour, Darwin and Dance." *Nature* 462, 288 (2009). https://doi.org/10.1038/462288a.

Graziano, Michael S. A. *God, Soul, Mind, Brain.* Teaticket, MA: LeapSci, 2010.

Green, Toby. "Africa in its fullness: The West focuses only on slavery, but the history of Africa is so much more than a footnote to European imperialism." https://aeon.co/essays/liberating-the-precolonial-history-of-africa.

Greenfield, Susan. *You and Me.* Devon, UK: Notting Hill, 2017.

Gregory, Brad S. *The Unintended Reformation.* Cambridge, MA: Belknap Press of Harvard University Press, 2012.

Griffith, Janelle. "Ahmaud Arbery shooting: A timeline of the case." https://www.nbcnews.com/news/us-news/ahmaud-arbery-shooting-timeline-case-n1204306.

Habl, Jan, and Jerry Root. *On Being Human.* Eugene, OR: Pickwick, 2017.

Harari, Yuval Noah. *Homo Deus: A Brief History of Tomorrow.* London: Vintage, 2018.

Harris, Sam. *Free Will.* New York: Free, 2012.

———. *Moral Landscape.* New York: Free, 2010.

Heidegger, Martin. *Basic Writings.* London: Harper Perennial, 2008.

Heilbroner, R. L., and Peter J. Boettke. "Economic system." https://www.britannica.com/topic/economic-system.

Henke, Joe. "Defense Attorneys Argue For Bond." https://www.11alive.com/article/news/crime/trials/travis-gregory-mcmichael-bond-hearing-ahmaud-arbery-case/85-27ee65bf-7026-4736-a795-51dfd05f62c0.

Hennigar, Adele. "Manipulate Aisthetika." http://www.adelehennigar.com/manipulate aisthetika.

Herdt, Jennifer A. *Putting On Virtue.* Chicago: University of Chicago Press, 2008.

Herrnstein, Richard J., and Charles Murray. *The Bell Curve.* New York: Free, 1996.

Hicks, Donna. *Dignity: Its Essential Role in Resolving Conflict.* New Haven, CT: Yale University Press, 2011.

Highfield, Ron. *God, Freedom, and Human Dignity.* Downers Grove, IL: IVP Academic, 2013.

Hilbink, Thomas M. "Omnibus Crime Control." https://www.encyclopedia.com/history/encyclopedias-almanacs-transcripts-and-maps/omnibus-crime-control-and-safe-streets-act-1968.

Hisham, Aidi. *Rebel Music.* New York: Vintage, 2014.

History.com.editors. "Emmett Till." https://www.history.com/topics/black-history/emmett-till-1.

Historyengine.richmond.edu. "Segregation Has Not Died." https://historyengine.richmond.edu/episodes/view/5305.

Hochschild, Adam. *King Leopold's Ghost.* New York: Mariner, 1998.

———. "Leopold II: King of Belgium." https://www.britannica.com/biography/Leopold-II-king-of-Belgium.

Horne, Gerald. *The Counter-Revolution of 1776.* New York: NYU Press, 2014.

Https://www.gilderlehrman.org/history-resources/teaching-resource/historical-context-facts-about-slave-trade-and-slavery.

Https://www.theguardian.com/theguardian/1999/may/13/features11.g22.

Hunter, James Davison. *To Change the World.* Oxford: Oxford University Press, 2010.

Hunter, Robert. "Governor reports on 1712 slave revolt." https://herb.ashp.cuny.edu/items/show/690.

Iep.utm.edu. "Social Contract Theory." https://iep.utm.edu/soc-cont/#SH2a.

Imamaliquotes.tumblr.com. "Your Savior." https://imamaliquotes.tumblr.com/post/77724351267/.

IMDb.com. "The Gray Ghost." https://www.imdb.com/title/tt0050021/.

Iqbal, Nosheen. "Interview: Academic Robin Diangelo." https://www.theguardian.com/world/2019/feb/16/white-fragility-racism-interview-robin-diangelo.

Jeffrey, James. "Remembering the black soldiers executed after Houston's 1917 race riot." https://www.pri.org/stories/2018-02-01/remembering-black-soldiers-executed-after-houstons-1917-race-riot.

Johnson, Bailey. "Laissez les Bon Temps Rouler!: Learn your Mardi Gras history." https://www.cbsnews.com/news/laissez-les-bon-temps-rouler-learn-your-mardi-gras-history/.

Kakade, Manasi. "Decode A Culture—Individualistic Vs. Collectivist." https://manasikakade.com/blog/2015/04/decode-a-culture-individualistic-vs-collectivist.

Kar, Sujita Kumar, and Meha Jain. "Current understandings about cognition and the neurobiological correlates in schizophrenia." https://pubmed.ncbi.nlm.nih.gov/27365960/n.

Karun, Philip. *Zen and the Art of Funk Capitalism.* Lincoln, NE: Writer's Showcase iUniverse, 2001.

Katongole, Emmanuel, and Chris Rice. *Reconciling All Things.* Downers Grove, IL: InterVarsity, 2008.

Kennedy, Randall. *Nigger: The Strange Career of a Troublesome Word.* New York: Vintage, 2003.

Khanga, Yelena, and Susan Jacoby. *Soul to Soul.* New York: Norton, 1992.

Kidney.org. "GFRF Calculator." https://www.kidney.org/professionals/kdoqi/gfr_calculator.

Kim, Eun Kyung. "Walter Scott shooting: Jury foreman explains how Michael Slager case resulted in mistrial." https://www.today.com/news/walter-scott-shooting-jury-foreman-explains-how-michael-slager-case-t105742.

King, Martin Luther, Jr. *Strength To Love.* Minneapolis: Fortress, 1981.

King, Tiffany Lethabo, et al. *Otherwise Worlds.* Durham, NC: Duke University Press, 2020.

Kraybill, Donald B. *The Upside-Down Kingdom.* Harrisonburg, VA: Herald, 2011.

Lanza, Robert, and Bob Berman. *Biocentrism.* Dallas: BenBella, 2009.

Latin-dictionary.net. "Ligo." https://latin-dictionary.net/definition/25678/ligo-ligare-ligavi-ligatus.

Lawrence, Bill. "The Scope of Police Questioning During a Routine Traffic Stop." https://ir.lawnet.fordham.edu/ulj/vol30/iss6/3.

Lerner, Michael. "Black Home Ownership Gap." https://www.washingtonpost.com/business/2020/07/23/black-homeownership-gap/?arc404=true.

Lewis, Danny. "Slave Revolt of 1712." https://www.smithsonianmag.com/smart-news/new-york-slave-revolt-1712-was-bloody-prelude-decades-hardship-180958665/.

Lexico.com. "Aesthetics." https://www.lexico.com/en/definition/aesthetics.

———. "Attitude." https://www.lexico.com/en/definition/attitude.

———. "Disdain." https://www.lexico.com/en/definition/disdain.

———. "Emotion." https://www.lexico.com/en/definition/emotion.

———. "Flashpoint." https://www.lexico.com/en/definition/flashpoint.

———. "Ology." https://www.lexico.com/en/definition/ology.

———. "Phrenology." https://www.lexico.com/en/definition/phrenology.

———. "Reconciliation." https://www.lexico.com/en/definition/reconciliation.

———. "Sociology." https://www.lexico.com/en/definition/sociology.

———. "Trade." https://www.lexico.com/en/definition/trade.

Lilla, Mark. *The Stillborn God*. New York: Vintage, 2007.

Lopez, Ian Haney. *White by Law*. New York: NYU Press, 2006.

Louth, Andrew. *The Origins of the Christian Mystical Tradition: From Plato to Denys*. Oxford: Oxford University Press, 2007.

Mao, Frances. "National Geographic apology: 'We were anticipated to be a dying race.'" https://www.bbc.com/news/world-australia-43410584.

Mayoclinic.org. "Carotid Artery disease." https://www.mayoclinic.org/diseases-conditions/carotid-artery-disease/symptoms-causes/syc-20360519.

McCluskey, Audrey Thomas. *Richard Pryor: The Life and Legacy of a "Crazy" Black Man*. Bloomington, IN: University of Indiana Press, 2008.

McKittrick, Katherine. *Sylvia Wynter: On Being Human as Praxis*. Durham, NC: Duke University Press, 2015.

McNulty, Ian. "Block Parties in Motion: the New Orleans Second Line Parade." https://www.frenchquarter.com/secondline/.

McWilliams, Nancy. "Projection." https://www.britannica.com/science/projection-psychology.

Meier, John P. *A Marginal Jew*. New York: Doubleday, 2001.

Merriam-Webster. "Human (noun)." https://www.merriam-webster.com/dictionary/human.

Mintz, Steven. "Historical Context: Facts about the Slave Trade and Slavery." https://www.gilderlehrman.org/history-resources/teaching-resource/historical-context-facts-about-slave-trade-and-slavery.

Monteiro ,Nicole M., and Diana J. Wall. "African Dance as Healing Modality Throughout the Diaspora: The Use of Ritual and Movement to Work Through Trauma." http://www.jpanafrican.org/docs/vol4no6/4.6-13AfricanDance.pdf.

Moseley, Alexander. "John Locke: Political Philosophy." https://iep.utm.edu.

MyJewishlearning.com. "This is Unity." https://www.myjewishlearning.com/article/this-is-unity/.

Napier, Winston. *African American Literary Theory*. New York: NYU Press, 2000.

Nationalhumanitiescenter.org. "Two views of the Stono Slave Rebellion." http://nationalhumanitiescenter.org/pds/becomingamer/peoples/text4/stonorebellion.pdf.

Nelson, Tom. *The Economics of Neighborly Love*. Downers Grove, IL: InterVarsity, 2017.

Nelsontreespecialist.com. "Can a Tree Grow Back Stump." https://www.nelsontreespecialist.com/blog/can-tree-grow-back-stump/.

Newkirk, Pamela. "The man who was caged in a zoo." https://www.theguardian.com/world/2015/jun/03/the-man-who-was-caged-in-a-zoo.

———. *Spectacle: The Astonishing Life of Ota Benga*. New York: Harper Collins, 2015.

Neworleans.com. "The Second Line: Buck-jumping for joy." https://www.neworleans.com/things-to-do/music/history-and-traditions/second-lines/.

Newworldencyclopedia.org. "African dance." https://www.newworldencyclopedia.org/entry/African_dance.

———. "Victor Turner." https://www.newworldencyclopedia.org/entry/Victor_Turner.

Nicholson, Graeme. *Justifying Our Existence*. Toronto: University Toronto Press, 2009.

Noble, Denis. *The Music of Life: Biology Beyond Genes*. Oxford: Oxford University Press, 2006.

Norman, Geoffrey. "What We Have Here Is Failure . . . to Miscommunicate." https://www.washingtonexaminer.com/weekly-standard/what-we-have-here-is-failure-to-miscommunicate.

Ostler, Scott. "Here's a Team That Changed Face of Game." https://www.latimes.com/archives/la-xpm-1989-01-25-sp-1058-story.html.

Oz, Amos, and Fania Oz-Salzberger. *Jews and Words*. New Haven, CT: Yale University Press, 2012.

Paris, Peter J. *A Spirituality of African Peoples*. Minneapolis: Fortress, 1995.

Pbs.org. "Logos." https://www.pbs.org/faithandreason/theogloss/logos-body.html.

———. "Meet the players: Other figures." https://www.pbs.org/wgbh/americanexperience/features/meet-players-other-figures/.

Pdinfo.com. "Public Domain Songs." https://www.pdinfo.com/pd-music-genres/pd-spirituals.php.

Pearsall, Paul. *The Heart's Code*. New York: Broadway, 1998.

Perry, Imani. *Prophets of the Hood*. Durham, NC: Duke University Press, 2004.

Peters, James R. *The Logic of the Heart: Augustine, Pascal, and the Rationality of Faith*. Grand Rapids: Baker Academic, 2009.

Petmd.com. "Staffordshire Bull Terrier." https://www.petmd.com/dog/breeds/c_dg_staffordshire_bull_terrier.

Pickman, Ben. "Drew Brees on NFL Players Kneeling: 'I Will Never Agree With Anybody Disrespecting the Flag.'" https://www.si.com/nfl/2020/06/03/saints-drew-brees-comments-kneeling-flag.

Podoksik, Ephraim. *The Cambridge Companion to Oakeshott*. Cambridge: Cambridge University Press, 2012.

Postrel, Virginia. "The Consequences of the 1960's Race Riots Come Into View." https://www.nytimes.com/2004/12/30/business/the-consequences-of-the-1960s-race-riots-come-into-view.html.

Prnewswire.com. "United States Weight Loss & Diet Control Market Report 2019." https://www.prnewswire.com/news-releases/united-states-weight-loss—diet-control-market-report-2019-2018-results—2019-2023-forecasts—-top-competitors-ranking-with-30-year-revenue-analysis-300803186.html.

Pvamu.edu. "1917 Houston riots camp Logan mutiny." https://www.pvamu.edu/tiphc/research-projects/the-1917-houston-riotscamp-logan-mutiny/.

Rebennack, Mac, and Jack Rummel. *Under a Hoodoo Moon*. New York: St. Martin's, 1994.

Richards, Keith. *Life*. New York: Hatchette, 2010.

Rohr, Richard. "Early Christian Values. "https://cac.org/early-christian-values-2015-04-27/.

Rollingstone.com. "500 Greatest Albums." https://www.rollingstone.com/music/music-lists/500-greatest-albums-of-all-time-156826/dr-john-dr-johns-gumbo-68237/.

Rosenzweig, Franz. *Star of Redemption*. Notre Dame, IN: University of Notre Dame Press, 2014.

Rothstein, Richard. *Color of Law*. New York: Liveright, 2017.

Rovelli, Carlo. *Reality Is Not What It Seems*. London: Penguin Random House, 2014.

Roy, Sanjoy. "How The Electric Slide became the Black Lives Matter protest dance." https://www.theguardian.com/stage/2020/jun/11/how-the-electric-slide-became-the-black-lives-matter-protest-dance.

Rutherford, Alan A. *A Brief History of Everyone Who Ever Lived.* London: Weidenfeld & Nicolson, 2017.

Sabar, Yona. "Hebrew word of the week: Gerim." https://jewishjournal.com/current_ edition/178191/.

Sacks, Jonathan. "The Dignity of Difference." The Office of Rabbi Sacks. https://rabbisacks. org/topics/stranger-2.

———. *The Home We Build Together.* London: Bloomsbury, 2007.

———. *To Heal A Fractured World.* New York: Schocken, 2005.

Sacks, Oliver. *Musicophilia: Tales of Music and the Brain.* New York: Vintage, 2008.

Saini, Angela. *Superior: The Return of Race Science.* Boston: Beacon, 2019.

Sandel, Michael J. *Justice: What is the Right Thing to Do.* New York: Farrar, Straus, and Giroux, 2009.

Schellekens, Elizabeth, and Peter Goldie. *The Aesthetic Mind.* Oxford: Oxford University Press, 2011.

Schulman, Bob. "Shake Your Booty." https://www.huffpost.com/entry/shake-your-booty-to-brukd_b_11282738?guccounter=1&guce_referrer=aHR0cHM6Ly 93d3cuZ29vZ2xlLmNvbVS8&guce_referrer_sig=AQAAAGOHjbhns6kj_Seku OYlCKXRJ7xpsqyI6pDBlOqPnPzB3DHXdJibDi5a89-0UNyyM4tnTLzAeps_ XlpFKdvRG44sdjipb5DYgDM-OjsRchkNAm1w5LKdUCf4w0EpU_QGxwsRrhA_ AMEzSZFu9HTR72-SDT9Oi5mWKt-_xdr3ln_I.

Scoutingwire.org. "Cub Scout Motto." https://scoutingwire.org/wp-content/uploads/ 2016/03/310-887C16_SPREAD-1.pdf.

Scruton, Roger. *On Human Nature.* Princeton, NJ: Princeton University Press, 2017.

———. *The Soul of the World.* Princeton, NJ: Princeton University Press, 2014.

Shapin, Steven. *Never Pure.* Baltimore: Johns Hopkins University Press, 2010.

Sherlockholmesquotes.com. http://sherlockholmesquotes.com.

Simkin, John. "Whipping of a Slave." https://spartacus-educational.com/USASwhipping. htm.

Sloan, Nate. "The Glorious Return of Funk." https://www.nytimes.com/interactive/ 2019/11/01/opinion/funk-music-returns.html.

Smith, Amanda. "The skull, the phrenologist and the solution to a 150-year-old mystery." https://www.abc.net.au/radionational/programs/archived/bodysphere/the-skull,- the-phrenologist-and-the-150-year-mystery/6636226.

Smith, Christian. *Moral Believing Animals: Personhood and Culture.* Oxford: Oxford University Press, 2003.

Smith, Douglas G. "Congenital Limb Deficiencies and Acquired Amputations in Childhood." https://www.amputee-coalition.org/resources/amputations-in-childhood/.

Smithsonian National Museum of African American History and Culture. "Newsweek November 1967." https://nmaahc.si.edu/object/nmaahc_201.17.

Sniderman, Paul M., and Louk Hagendoorn. *When Ways of Life Collide.* Princeton, NJ: Princeton University Press, 2007.

Spiked-online. "John Hume." https://www.spiked-online.com/2020/08/04/how-john-hume-paved-the-way-for-peace/.

Stassen, Glen H., and David P. Gushee. *Kingdom Ethics.* Downers Grove, IL: InterVarsity, 2003.

Statista.com. "Health & Fitness Clubs Statistics & Facts." https://www.statista.com/ topics/1141/health-and-fitness-clubs/.

Stoller-Conrad, Jessica. "Why Did Western Europe Dominate the Globe?" https://www.caltech.edu/about/news/why-did-western-europe-dominate-globe-47696.

Supunsala, Dinushi. "Color Symbolism (part 1)." https://dinushisupunsala.medium.com/color-symbolism-part1-9e4651816a16.

Sutherland, Claudia. "Stono Rebellion (1739)." https://www.blackpast.org/african-american-history/stono-rebellion-1739/.

Swinburne, Richard. *Mind, Brain, and Free Will.* Oxford: Oxford University Press, 2013.

Taleb, Nassim Nicholas. *Skin in the Game: Hidden Asymmetries in Daily Life.* New York: Random House, 2018.

Tanev, Stoyan, and David Bradshaw. *Energy in Orthodox Theology and Physics.* Eugene, OR: Pickwick, 2017.

Thisisafrica.me. "What Africa Had Before Colonisation." https://thisisafrica.me/african-identities/africa-colonisation/.

Thompson, Dave. *Funk.* San Francisco: Backbeat, 2001.

Thu, Sumyat. "Anti-blackness: A World Problem We Are All Connected To." https://seattleglobalist.com/2016/07/26/anti-blackness-world-problem/54274.

Tull, Matthew. "Hypervigilance With PTSD and Other Anxiety Disorders." https://www.verywellmind.com/hypervigilance-2797363%2016.

Turner, Edith. *Experiencing Ritual: A New Interpretation of African Healing.* Philadelphia: University of Pennsylvania Press, 1992.

Tutu, Desmond. *An African Prayer Book.* New York: Doubleday, 1995.

University of Jyväskylä—Jyväskylän yliopisto. "The way you dance is unique, and computers can tell it's you." www.sciencedaily.com/releases/2020/01/200117104740.htm.

Uwagba, Otegha. *Whites: On Race and Other Falsehoods.* London: 4th Estate, 2020.

Vincent, Ricky. *Funk: The Music of the People.* New York: St. Martin's, 1996.

Visual-arts-cork.com. "Paris Salon." http://www.visual-arts-cork.com/history-of-art/salon-paris.htm#history.

Vocabulary.com. "Funk." https://www.vocabulary.com/dictionary/funk.

Wade, Peter. *Race: An Introduction.* Cambridge: Cambridge University Press, 2015.

Walden, Lisa. "Staffies and Westies have been revealed as the most affectionate dog breeds." https://www.countryliving.com/uk/wildlife/dog-breeds/a27328818/affectionate-dog-breeds-staffies-westies/.

Walford, John. *Great Themes in Art.* Upper Saddle River, NJ: Prentice-Hall, 2002.

Walker, Alice, and Zora Neal Hurston. *Barracoon: The Story of the Last "Black Cargo."* New York: Amistad, 2020.

Walsh, John. "Austen power: 200 years of Pride and Prejudice." https://www.independent.co.uk/arts-entertainment/books/features/austen-power-200-years-pride-and-prejudice-8454448.html.

Ward, Graham. *The Politics of Discipleship.* Grand Rapids: Baker Academic, 2009.

Warren, Michael. "American Survival Guide." http://www.americassurvivalguide.com/thomas_hobbes.php.

Watson, Peter. *Convergence.* New York: Simon & Shuster, 2016.

Watson, Rebecca, and Beatrice de Gelder. "How White and Black Bodies Are Perceived Depends on What Emotion Is Expressed." https://www.nature.com/articles/srep41349#Sec6.

Watson, Richard A. *Solipsism: The Ultimate Theory of Human Existence.* South Bend, IN: St. Augustine's, 2016.

Weiss, Raymond L., and Charles Butterworth. *Ethical Writings of Maimonides*. New York: Dover, 1975.

Welsh, Kim. "Jazz, From Funky Butt Hall to Carnegie Hall." https://frenchquarterly.com/music/jazz-funky-butt-hall-carnegie-hall.

West, Cornel. *The Cornel West Reader*. New York: Basic Civitas, 2010.

Wikipedia.org. "Gumbo." https://en.wikipedia.org/wiki/Gumbo.

Wilder, Amos N. *Theopoetic: Theology and the Religious Imagination*. Eugene, OR: Wipf & Stock, 2013.

Wilson, Timothy B. *Strangers to Ourselves: Discovering the Adaptive Conscious*. Cambridge, MA: Belknap Press of Harvard University Press, 2003.

Wnyc.org. "All You Need is a Loaded Gun: Black Panther Party Funk." https://www.wnyc.org/story/the-lumpen-black-panther-party-funk/.

Wolfe, Gregory. *Beauty Will Save the World*. Wilmington, DE: ISI, 2011.

Wolterstorff, Nicholas. *Art in Action*. Grand Rapids: Eerdmans, 1980.

Yetman, Norman R. *Voices from Slavery*. Mineola, NY: Dover, 2000.

Young, Jennifer. "Persistent Racism of America's Cemeteries." https://www.atlasobscura.com/articles/the-persistent-racism-of-americas-cemeteries.

Youtube.com. "Clifford Coulter." https://www.youtube.com/watch?v=YPUhuhfoAjo.